MASERATI ROAD CARS

MASERATI
ROAD CARS

The postwar production cars 1946 to 1979

Richard Crump and Rob de la Rive Box

Osprey

Published in 1979
by Osprey Publishing Limited
12–14 Long Acre, London
WC2E 9LP
Member company of the
George Philip Group

British Library Cataloguing
in Publication Data
Crump, Richard
Maserati road cars.
1. Maserati automobile
I. Title   II. Box, Rob de la Rive
629.22′22   TL.215.M34

ISBN 0-9530721-8-5

Editor: Tim Parker
Design: Claydon · Hook · Mann

Facsimile reprint 1999, with kind permission of the original publishers.

Published by Mercian Manuals
353 Kenilworth Road
Balsall Common
Coventry CV7 7DL

CONTENTS

FOREWORD

In a late 1977 edition of the *New Yorker*, the American East Coast's 'society' magazine, there was a full page cartoon depicting a function in something which resembled a ballroom. In the foreground was a tall, thin, aristocratic-looking young man facing a nearly as tall and thin but somewhat more elderly lady in a flowing gown. 'What do you do?' she was asking him. 'I drive a Maserati' was the reply.

Doug Blain, one-time editor of England's sometimes outspoken *CAR* magazine once wrote that as a youth he dreamed about Maseratis. My guess is that it must have been round about the time that the 250F grand prix car was winning races in various hands perhaps, in particular, those of Stirling Moss. Blain went on to explain that he liked the sound of the name— Maser *rat* ti.

Pop singer Joe Walsh sings a strange song entitled *Life's been good* into the 'Top Twenty'. One line bleats through all the others; 'My Maserati does one-eighty-five.' 185 km/h? Hardly enough to boast about. 185 mph, unlikely!

What you may ask is so special about each one of the anecdotes above? Each one tells a little 'Maserati' tale and there is no lack of those. But that misses the point. If you were to replace the word Maserati in each with either Ferrari or Lamborghini would not each tale still be worth telling? The answer is positively 'no'. Each one summarises the fascination and the mystique of a type that only *Il Tridente* can produce.

Peter Coltrin, long time American in Modena, correspondent to so many motoring magazines throughout the world, once wrote 'I doubt if a truly definitive history of the Maserati operations can ever be written. It is a long and rather complicated history . . .', (*Motor*, 10 July 1971). Four company owners, numerous financial peaks and troughs and over thirty years of historical neglect have left little for the enthusiast to chew over with any real hope of unravelling the truth. Our business is to deal with truth and consequently that makes books of this type hard to produce.

MASERATI ROAD CARS, for the first time, sorts out the company's production cars into an acceptable assembly, giving their specifications directly from company brochures and build sheets, their production figures from company orders and invoices, and their development from other company archives, interviews, handbooks, photographs and analysis of previously suspect material. If there are mistakes and misinterpretations, and there certainly will be some for no book dealing with such a diverse subject can ever be free, they are made because even we did not suspect the substance of their content.

We have given the facts as we see them, of that there is no question. What we have also tried to do is to come to terms with the charisma, mystique and aura of the Maserati through the design of the book.

What is that precious quality which has enabled Maserati to survive so many attacks against its very being while constantly in the Ferrari shadow and sometimes lacking the Lamborghini glamour? There may be some explanation here.

Osprey Publishing
23 August 1979

INTRODUCTION

8

In 1937 Comm. Adolfo Orsi founder and head of the Orsi Group (Orsi SAS) purchased a controlling interest in the Maserati works at Bologna, although a year later it was moved to Modena. The Orsi empire had financial interests in iron works, machine tool manufacture, agricultural machinery, spark plugs and controlled several city tramways and railroads in Italy. There was a ten year business agreement between Orsi and the Maserati brothers, at the end of which the Maserati family decided to withdraw, return again to Bologna to start another small company, O.S.C.A., (or Officina Specializzata Costruzione Automobili). Orsi's new company, Officine Alfieri Maserati, was started in 1947 and Adolfo handed the reins to his very young but serious son Omer Orsi. Although the Orsi Group employed several thousand people there were a mere thirty employees in the car/racing factory at Modena. Omer contracted the services of Ing.Gorrin, Ing.Massimino and Ing.Bellentani, the last two from Ferrari, to design the immediate postwar competition and subsequent Maserati production cars. In 1951, engineers Massimino and Gorrini left to be replaced by Colombo from Alfa Romeo, and eventually in late 1955, by Dr. Ing.Alfieri.

Orsi retained control of the Maserati factory until 1969 when he sold a major interest to Société Citroën who were at the time looking for an engine development company for their forthcoming SM project, and a prestige automobile manufacturer. Later on in 1971, Omer Orsi pulled-out altogether owing to a disagreement with the French management over their future policies.

During the third week of May 1975, Citroën announced from their Paris offices that it was preparing to put the Maserati factory into voluntary liquidation. Reasons for this were numerous; the losses of 1974 exceeded the entire share capital of the company and undoubtedly the SM never reached the sales heights anticipated by Citroën (engine production was, therefore, uneconomic), plus Maserati cars were just not selling well in the luxury car market. Production at the time was around ten to fifteen cars and 120 engines per month, most of the engines being the V6 unit. The 700 factory personnel had been on short time since the beginning of 1975 and Citroën, who had problems of their own, felt no longer able to underwrite the loss of the Modena company. By announcing its intention to liquidate Maserati, the French company were simultaneously looking for a possible buyer who could relieve their pressures. During that year many automobile manufacturers were experiencing disappointing sales of all their cars, so neither state-owned Alfa Romeo nor the Fiat group (Fiat, Lancia, Ferrari) were interested in such a rescue operation.

By the beginning of June 1975, talks began with

9

Il Tridente—Located in Bologna's Piazza del Nettuno, specially opened by the order of Pius IV in 1564, is the Fontana del Nettuno (Neptune's or 'the giant's' fountain). This fountain was designed by Tommaso Laureati of Palermo and adorned with bronze sculptures by Giambologna (Jean Boulogne) in 1566. At the top Neptune with trident is in the act of appeasing the waves and below are infants with dolphins and sinuous sirens with their heads framed by jewelled stoles. The marble parts were the work of Giovanni Andrea della Porta, Ant. Fasana and And. Riva.

It is this distinctively shaped trident head that inspired its adoption as the symbol for Officine Alfieri Maserati SpA right at the beginning. The red and blue of the Maserati badge are traditional Bologna colours

Alessandro de Tomaso who could obviously see integration possibilities with the De Tomaso Group which consisted of Innocenti (Societa Generale per l'Industria Metallurgica e Meccanica, Milan), Fratelli Benelli SpA, Moto Guzzi and, of course, Automobiles de Tomaso. After some six months of talks a transaction was concluded in December 1975 for De Tomaso and GEPI to purchase Maserati from the French company. The major stockholder was GEPI, the Italian government agency concerned mainly with the use of labour. In partnership, De Tomaso, who had a thirty per cent holding was responsible for the day-to-day running of the company; the Maserati factory was saved from liquidation and the workers, although greatly reduced in numbers, returned in 1976. The new design team was to be controlled by Ing.Casarini while Aurelio Bertocchi was made general manager of Maserati, a position he already held with the De Tomaso car factory. Also to return was Omer Orsi, as commercial director, although he eventually resigned finally from the Maserati board in late 1977.

For a brief moment *The Legend* hesitated once more in 1975, but after the previous fifty years it was no great surprise and certainly no great disgrace. Maserati continue to produce fine automobiles and magnificent engines into the late nineteen seventies. *The Legend* continues. . . .

Omer Orsi happily sitting in one of his first series of sports racing cars, the A6GCS, at the factory in 1951

10

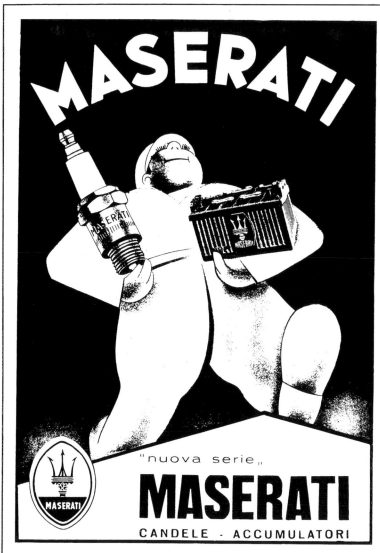

An advertisement from a 1948 issue of *Motor Italia* promoting only the company's batteries and spark plugs. This one was not printed in colour although it occupied a whole page measuring some 8·25 inches across by 11·25 inches deep

One year later, using the same magazine, Maserati decided that their cars needed advertising and that the use of colour was desirable. This was a four colour printing—red, blue, black and yellow (the yellow being under the red of the heading 'MASERATI')

The home of Maserati spark plugs, batteries and motorcycles on the outskirts of Modena, owned by the Orsi family in the mid-1950s

Metalmeccanici oggi in agitazione per solidarietà con la Maserati

Le proposte dei liquidatori ai sindacati nell'incontro di ieri Gli operai le respingono - Delegazione delle maestranze modenesi a Parigi per un incontro con i sindacati francesi

DIREZIONE CITROEN = FALLIMENTO

Uno dei tanti cartelli appesi alla recinzione della Maserati. Le critiche sono tutte per i dirigenti francesi della gloriosa casa automobilistica condotta all'orlo della disgregazione.

Oggi le aziende metalmeccaniche modenesi si fermeranno alle ore 16. Non si tratta di un vero e proprio sciopero ma di una grande manifestazione di solidarietà per i colleghi della Maserati. Il lavoro viene sospeso per permettere a tutti i lavoratori metalmeccanici della provincia di raggiungere alle ore 18 la Piazza Grande dove avrà luogo una manifestazione di solidarietà nel corso della quale parleranno il sindaco dott. Germano Bulgarelli, il presidente del Consiglio di fabbrica della Maserati, Franco Facchini ed i sindacalisti. Ieri si è appreso che nei prossimi giorni una delegazione di operai della Maserati tornerà a Parigi, dove è stata qualche giorno fa, per un altro incontro con una rappresentanza sindacale francese della stessa categoria, in vista di un'azione comune contro la Citroen a sostegno del complesso modenese controlato appunto dalla fabbrica automobilistica francese.

Un lunghissimo incontro, intanto, è avvenuto ieri alla Associazione Industriali tra i rappresentanti dei sindacati, dei dipendenti della Maserati e colui che sembra essere il presidente del collegio dei tre liquidatori, Colombani. Nel corso della seduta, che si è protratta per diverse ore, Colombani, preso atto che la Citroen ha accettato la messa in cassa integrazione dei dipendenti, ha formulato diverse proposte, valide per tre settimane, secondo i poteri a lui conferiti dal collegio dei liquidatori. A partire da lunedì prossimo i dipendenti lavoreranno due giorni alla settimana in numero ridotto: 295 operai e 72 impiegati già scelti, a detta di Colombani, secondo motivazioni tecniche di reparto. Gli altri dipendenti rimarranno a casa e percepiranno regolarmente quanto loro dovuto dalla Cassa integrazione guadagni. Dopo le tre settimane, che coincidono pressapoco con la data del 25 giugno, allorchè si avrà al ministero dell'Industria il secondo incontro dei sindacati e della Citroen col ministro Donat Cattin, la Cassa integrazione sarà conferita a « ore zero », rimanendo l'azienda aperta tutti i giorni con soli 34 operai e 19 impiegati per il reparto addetti al servizio clienti.

I sindacalisti presenti hanno preso nota dei progetti dell'azienda e si sono riservati di dare una risposta in una prossima riunione che avrà luogo alle ore 16 di martedì prossimo presso l'Associazione Industriali. Nel tardo pomeriggio i sindacalisti hanno indetto una assemblea di fabbrica nel corso della quale hanno riferito sulle proposte del liquidatore Colombani. Si ha notizia chè i dipendenti le avrebbero respinte, ribadendo che non intendono rimanere a casa e percepire il relativo compenso senza lavorare.

Nel tardo pomeriggio inoltre il segretario della Cisl, Arletti, è partito improvvisamente per Roma, dove, si dice, avrà colloqui con il ministro Donat Cattin per renderlo edotto delle proposte della Citroen.

Il dott. Giorgi, direttore dell'Associazione Industriali, che ha partecipato alle trattative, ha reso noto di avere già avviato, richiedendo la procedura d'urgenza, la pratica per conto della Citroen della messa dei dipendenti in Cassa integrazione. E' stato reso noto inoltre che i dipendenti della Citroen verranno a Modena nella prossima settimana per rendersi conto della situazione. In questa situazione pessimistica si spera, comunque, di riuscire a sbloccare la situazione di stallo attuale, ammesso che un compratore si sia fatto avanti concretamente. Fino a una decina di giorni fa, il nome che ricorreva di più era qello di Alessandro De Tomaso. Ultimamente di un passaggio dell'azienda al «manager» sudamericano non si è più parlato. Non si esclude, tuttavia, che non siano in corso trattative nel riserbo.

Cronaca di Modena, Thursday 5 June 1975 'Direzione Citroën = Fallimento'

In the pits at the Modena test track in 1953, Orsi appears to be concerned while his A6GCM Formula 2 car undergoes routine testing

A sight never to be seen again? Five Indys on their way to the United Kingdom by French transporter stopped en route. The year? Probably 1971 or 1972. Cars are now delivered singly or collected by their new owners

13

Daily Express, Friday 30 May 1975 'It was more than a motor car; it was a legend.'

Motoring's legends fight to survive

By Ray Heath

THE sharp profit set-back at Ford is further evidence of the malaise among mass motor manufacturers.

Volkswagen, British Leyland and Chrysler are already casualties of the oil crisis.

Its combined effects of a world-wide recession and higher petrol prices have hit the motor industry hardest.

All these mass manufacturers expect to stay in business, but can the super-luxury makers survive? Are we about to see the end of the great and glamorous names which are part of motoring history?

Almost unnoticed, Maserati has just closed down. It was more than a motor car; it was a legend.

The survivors reckon they can fight back. All struggle on hoping that enough con-

	Number of cars per year	Number of employees	Cars per worker each year
BRISTOL	about 300	100	3+
FERRARI	1,800	800	1·8
JENSEN	1,820	700	2·6
LAMBORGHINI	800	850	1
MASERATI	130	800	0·16
PORSCHE	11,500	3,000	3·8

❛ People still want exclusive cars ❜

—TONY CROOK OF BRISTOL CARS

noisseurs will still have the money to keep them in business.

Only the two biggest performance car specialists, Group Lotus and Porsche, have bowed to the wind of economic change by stressing the economy of their products.

Others, including Bristol, Lamborghini and the Fiat-controlled Ferrari, defy the usual laws of motor industry economics.

They believe they can keep a top slice of the market so long as they do not make their cars commonplace. People will still buy a car just

because it is the most expensive.

"People still want a very exclusive car," said Bristol's chairman, Tony Crook. "A lot of people like to have something made properly."

For Bristol's cachet of exclusiveness they are prepared to pay up to £14,500.

Mr. Crook, a former speed record-breaker, in Bristol cars, reckons the secret of staying alive in the luxury car business is finding the right niche and staying in it.

"I would not like to make more than six cars a week. Two years ago, when you could sell anything with wheels, we could have doubled or trebled production. But then we would have been into a different concept of motoring," he said.

So production at the company's Filton factory has gone on steadily and loyal customers keep coming from all over the world.

The problems Bristol avoided by staying small are illustrated by Jensen the West Bromwich maker of grand touring and sports cars. Jensen, controlled by American car sales ace Kjell Qvale, has cut its weekly production down to 10 Interceptors and 25 Healeys. At one time last year, it was making 25 Interceptors and 100 Healeys a week.

The cuts have reduced the workforce from 1,200 to around 700, but the worst seems to be over. Jensen's sales are now around 16% higher than in the first few months of this year, said director Tony Good.

Porsche, whose top model sells for £15,000 in Britain, also expects to recover this year.

The company, controlled by the founder's son, Dr. Ferry Porsche, sold 11,500 cars last year but made profits of only £80,000.

This year it plans to build "at least" 10,000 cars and expects to make higher profits.

Porsche is lucky because its research and development side sells space-age technology to the world's motor industry.

❛ You've got to stay small ❜

—LAMBORGHINI AGENT

While Ferrari fell into the arms of Fiat, its younger high-performance rival, Lamborghini, is still independent of the big groups.

Last year it was taken over by two Swiss business men, George Henri Rosetti and René Liemer.

Their cash-backing has given the company enough confidence to set up an extensive new model programme.

It is producing 800 sleek roadsters a year and, like Bristol, plans to keep going by staying small.

"By keeping the number small you survive," said Lamborghini's U.K. agent Roger

PRODUCTION NOTES

Production figures given in this book, for each model, are the result of in-depth research into the build sheets and other records made available at the Maserati factory. It is not certain that these figures are one hundred per cent accurate, in fact, it would be fair to say that they very firmly are not. However, they are as accurate as it is possible to make them. Not all records were looked at, for a number of reasons, and it should be appreciated that small, low-volume specialist manufacturers, especially those in Italy, tend to keep a closed door on their records—Maserati is no exception.

Postwar production engine family tree

Omer Orsi confirms that this table is indicative of the progression of models since the commencement of postwar production. That there are variations on this theme is common knowledge but this table notes the important announcements.

voiturette	Tipo 6CM	6-cylinder (65 × 75 mm) twin-cam introduced mid-1936. Maserati brothers design
production sports	A6/1500	6-cylinder (66 × 72·5 mm) single came introduced 1947. Orsi period commences
racing	A6GCS	6-cylinder (72 × 81 mm) single cam introduced September 1947
production sports	A6G/2000	6-cylinder (72 × 80 mm) single cam introduced 1951
racing	A6GCS	6-cylinder (72 × 81 mm) twin-cam introduced 1951
Formula 2 sports	A6GCM	6-cylinder (75 × 75 mm) twin-cam introduced early 1952
racing	A6GCS	6-cylinder (76·5 × 72 mm) twin-cam introduced early 1953
production	A6G/2000	6-cylinder (76·5 × 72 mm) twin-cam introduced early 1954
production	3500	developed from 1956 sports racing model Tipo 350S. 6-cylinder (86 × 100 mm) twin-cam introduced early 1957
production	5000	developed from 1956 sports racing model Tipo 450S. 8-cylinder (98·5 × 81 mm) four-cam introduced late 1959

From the 3500 design, Ing. Alfieri developed the 3700 unit for use in the Sebring (GTIS), which in turn was stretched again for the 4000 Mistral. Conversely the basic 5000 engine design was linered and destroked to give capacities of 4200, 4700 and 4900 for use in the Quattroporte I, Mexico, Ghibli, Indy, Bora and Khamsin. The V6 engine for the Merak was a redesign of the Maserati unit used in the Citroën SM.

15

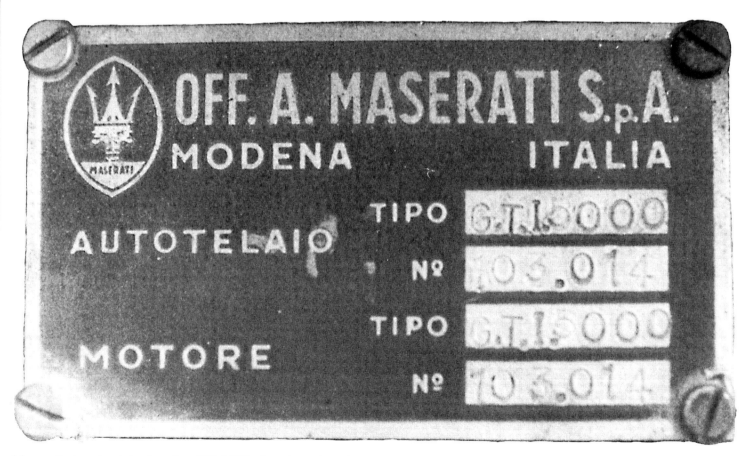

Maserati chassis plate showing GTI 5000 chassis and engine designations. Both are numbered 103.014, the seventh car in the 5000GT series

Chassis and engine plate identification

This is a list of the identification prefixes stamped on the chassis and engine plates. Four or five digits were stamped after the prefix full point given in the centre column. The AM plate, representing Officine Alfieri Maserati, was screwed either to the bulkhead or side panels inside the engine compartment. Plates were either red or green with the exception of the 1500 and 2000 cc models which had two separate tags similar to the sports-racing cars. Engine numbers were also stamped on the cylinder head and on top of the clutch housing at the rear of the block. Chassis numbers were on a plate welded to the top of a front wishbone.

6-cylinder 1500	A6/1500.	consecutive
6-cylinder	A6G/2000.	consecutive
3500 coupé	AM101.	alternate even
3500 spider	AM101.	alternate odd
Sebring 3500	AM101/10.	alternate odd
Sebring 3700	AM101/S/10.	alternate odd
Sebring 4000	AM101/A/10.	alternate odd
Mistral 3700	AM109.	alternate even
Mistral 4000	AM109/A1.	alternate even
Mistral 3500 spider	AM109/S.	alternate odd
Mistral 3700 spider	AM109/S1.	alternate odd
Mistral 4000 spider	AM109/SA1.	alternate odd
5000GT	AM103.	
Quattroporte 4200	AM107.	
Quattroporte 4700	AM107/47.	
Mexico 4200	AM112.	
Mexico 4700	AM112/1.	
Ghibli 4700	AM115.	
Ghibli 4700 spider	AM115/S.	alternate odd
Ghibli 4900 SS	AM115/49.	
Ghibli SS 4900 spider	AM115/S/49.	alternate odd
Indy 4200	AM116.	
Indy 4700	AM116/47.	
Indy 4900	AM116/49.	
Bora 4700	AM 117.	
Bora 4900	AM 117/49.	
Merak	AM 122.	alternate even
Merak SS	AM 122/SS.	alternate even
Merak 2000	AM 122/D.	alternate even
Khamsin	AM 120.	
Quattroporte II	AM 123.	alternate even
Kyalami	AM 129.	alternate even

Note The 5000GT chassis plate which is illustrated shows that there is a full point between the AM103 prefix and its following number. Full points were not always used—sometimes it could have been a colon or an oblique line depending on what stamping tool was available at the time.

Apart from the Ghibli spider, all V8 chassis numbers were in even numbers for left-hand drive cars and in odd numbers for right-hand drive cars.

The Merak 2000 is available in Italy only, with left-hand drive.

Derivation of the model names

SEBRING Named after the factory's competition association with this famous American airfield racing circuit. (*Pronounced ce-bring*)

MISTRAL A north west wind blowing from land to sea in the area of the Gulf of Leone on the French Mediterranean coast

QUATTROPORTE The Italian for 'four door'

MEXICO To commemorate the Grand Prix win of the Cooper-Maserati driven by John Surtees in Mexico during the 1966 season

GHIBLI A collection of winds blowing in the Sahara desert. (*Pronounced gee-blee*)

INDY A belated acknowledgement to the Grand Prix Maserati's two wins in the Indianapolis 500 race in 1939 and 1940

BORA A very strong north by north west wind blowing from land (Trieste) towards the north Adriatic sea

MERAK The second star of the constellation of the Plough. (*Pronounced mey-rack*)

KHAMSIN A hot, violent gale which blows across the Sahara each year. It can last up to two months at a time. (*Pronounced cam sin*)

[KYALAMI] (A De Tomaso car in all but name and engine. Named after the famous South African racing circuit in recognition of the Cooper-Maserati victory, driven by Pedro Rodriguez, in the 1967 South African Grand Prix)

Production Notes

Year by year and cumulative production

	Year by year	Cumulative	
1946	2	2	
1947	3	5	
1948	9	14	
1949	23	37	
1950	23	60	
1951 } 1952 } 1953 }	16	76	
1954	4	80	
1955	12	92	
1956	34	126	
1957	15	141	
1958	122	263	
1959	200	463	
1960	456	919	
1961	534	1453	
1962	497	1950	
1963	633	2583	
1964	355	2938	
1965	448	3386	
1966	387	3773	
1967	600	4373	
1968	675	5048	
1969	483	5531	**Orsi period**
1970	544	6075	
1971	472	6547	
1972	577	7124	
1973	670	7714	
1974	495	8209	
1975	338	8547	**Citroën period**
1976	34(?)	8581(?)	
1977	249	8830	
1978	289	9119	**De Tomaso period***

* No Merak 3000 figure is given for 1976 and the 110 Kyalamis of 1977 and 1978 are not included.

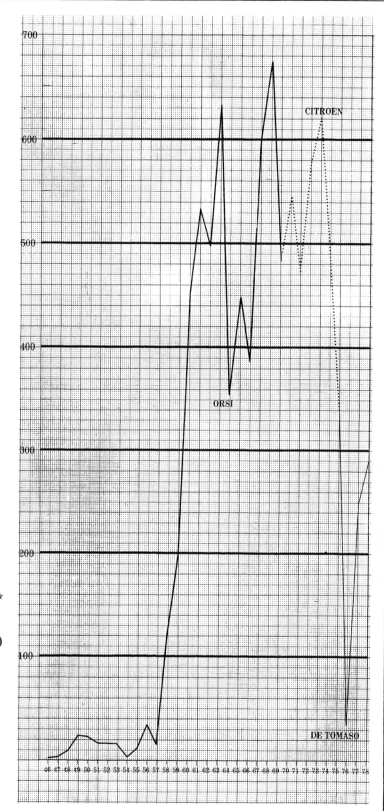

17

PART·1

The small capacity sixes—1946 to 1957

By increasing the bore of the 6CM *motore* 1 mm and the stroke 2·5 mm Orsi's inherited Fratelli Maserati design could be used as the basis for his planned 1500 cc production car engine. A cast iron block and detachable cylinder head fitted with single chain drive camshaft, wet sump lubrication, single ignition and one twin-choke Weber DVL-35 carburettor were the feature of this dull in-line six, from which was claimed 65 bhp at a peak of 5700 rpm with a compression ratio of 7·8 to 1. A four speed gearbox of Orsi's own design, single-plate clutch and bevel gear rear axle were mounted in an oval tube frame with cross-bracing in the centre section. The factory announced this model as the A6/1500 and exhibited it at the 1947 Geneva Motor Show. Such journalistic phrases as 'elegant, pleasing, attractive and simple' greeted this Pinin Farina coupé.

I suppose if you really favoured the beautiful 1947 Cisitalia coupé, then you would welcome this first Maserati 'road car'.

Pinin Farina was the only coachbuilder for the A6/1500 between 1946 and 1950, and during that period a total of 61 cars were completed. From research at the factory it would seem that Orsi actually finished two coupés in 1946, bearing chassis numbers 051 and 052, although they were not, of course, shown in that year. It must now be considered remarkable that they could produce any automobiles at all under the difficult circumstances which still prevailed in the postwar gloom of northern Italy.

While Froilen Gonzalez was giving the new twin-ignition Formula 2 A6GCM a second place in the 1952 Italian Grand Prix at Monza, a certain Signor Fezzardi was adding his piece of glory to the Maserati score board. Driving a 1947 Pinin Farina A6/1500 coupé this gentleman led the 1·5-litre class in the Fourth Coppa Inter-Europa for sports cars, eventually finishing second to Count Lurani's factory-entered Porsche. Competitive motoring for these early Maserati coupés was not, somehow, encouraged by the salesmen of the day, and this may well have been an isolated although successful instance.

In 1950 Zagato bodied a Fiat 750 with his 'Panoramic' coachwork, the side windows and windscreen-top curved into the body contours, but the car's rear-end treatment was very close to the first Maserati coupé. Perhaps as time passes these early Maseratis will begin to receive the credit due to them.

In 1951, the cubic capacity of the A6/1500 was increased by half a litre, although the single camshaft cylinder head configuration was retained. The Italian sun must have been prevalent during this era as both Pinin Farina and Pietro Frua offered their individual ideas of a cabriolet Maserati. Gross production of the single cam 2-litre sixes was no more than sixteen cars, and from this laughable statistic it can be rightly assumed that the factory were heavily engaged in other activities. Those were their sports racing and Formula 2 cars; it was almost as if the Maserati brothers' original attitude prevailed towards the building of a road car, neither one-off nor production model appeared to go hand in hand on a Maserati factory floor. It was very unlikely that Orsi was sure if what he was marketing as a road car was saleable or not, his energies being temporarily thwarted by the racing scene. However, during 1952 the economic bell sounded and Omer Orsi began to persuade himself that running a racing team needed money other than from his own pocket, and that the money should come from the sales of a production car.

After leaving Alfa Romeo in August 1952, Comm. Gioacchino Colombo joined the team of Ing. Luigi Bellantani and Alberto Massimino at the Maserati factory to work on a new series of the A6GCS. Ing. Massimino had been at Modena since the early postwar days and was already credited with the single cam A6GCS design and the Tipo A6GCM Formula 2 car. For Omer Orsi, the 2-litre sports racing car was to become a winner both in terms of track success and company profit. It enabled him to market an off-the-shelf competition model for less than £4000 and at the same time deploy a high proportion of factory resources and personnel towards a regular production series. From 1953 to 1955 the factory constructed 46 examples of this A6GCS series, plus some variation based on the same chassis, and it is now considered by many enthusiasts to be one of the best looking mid-fifties sports cars. It was, therefore, both understandable and practical that Orsi use the A6GCS as a springboard for his production car plans, a direction in which he had to go in order for his formula racing cars to be built and entered for world wide competition long term. It was not financially possible for Orsi interests to operate the factory for the exclusive use of building racing cars, as their return on capital investment would have been too meagre.

Through late 1953, besides their commitment to the A6GCS, engineers Colombo and Bellentani put their efforts into designing a milder form of the sports racing engine and this materialized in time for the Geneva Motor Show in March 1954. Power output of the A6GCS in 1953 was reckoned to be 160 bhp but after a hard first season of competition it was gradually tweaked to give 165 bhp, and by late 1954 was quoted to be developing 170 bhp at 7500 rpm. Retaining the basic aluminium block with its dry, cast iron liners and same bore and stroke dimensions, the Maserati engineers designed a new cylinder head, camshafts and pistons altering the compression ratio to 8·0 to 1. Probably through his association with Vittorio Jano while at Alfa Romeo, Colombo dispensed with the finger actuated valve gear and incorporated a screw type tappet arrangement with chain drive twin camshafts. The dry sump was replaced with wet sump lubrication and the oil filler cast in between the camshaft housings. Ignition for the six plug engine was by single Marelli ST65 distributor, electrics were 12 volt and the dynamo armature shaft was geared to the water pump and as one unit clamped on the side of the block beneath the exhaust manifolds. Power was supposedly 150 bhp at 6000 rpm but I would think a more realistic figure for those first series engines would have been 140 bhp at a peak of 6000 rpm on a lower compression ratio of 7·6 to 1. All engines were bench tested to maximum revs and at some time during the dynamometer test each unit was throttled instantly to ensure it could attain maximum revs without hesitation. The time devoted to each engine once assembled was eight hours, including the dyno test for ignition, carburation and valve settings. It would seem as though the factory had every intention of building the production units with specific attention to detail using the practices learned in their racing department.

The Geneva Show car was given the designation A6G/2000, on some build sheets A6G/54G.T., and was shown as a spacious, all aluminium, two door coupé with coachwork by Pietro Frua of Turin. This coachbuilder in fact entitled his creation 'Maserati 2000 Coupé Gran Sport' and this nameplate appeared either side of the front wings. It was reported at the time by some of the motoring press that this new model received a low reception from the public and interested customers, who were of the opinion that it was merely a coachbuilt A6GCS and consequently unsuitable for everyday use. Exactly what the public relations people at Modena did about this is not known but by the Paris Salon some months later, public reaction to the A6G/2000 had changed. It may have been due to the then newly appointed Maserati importer for France, M. Thepenier of Paris who, with Colonel John Simone, commenced his association with the factory which was to continue for more than twenty years. In the December 1954 issue of *Motor Racing* after a ride through the Bois de Boulogne, Hans Tanner wrote about this particular car that its acceleration was instantaneous, roadholding faultless although the ride was choppy and its manouverability was excellent. With Simone driving they attempted some acceleration tests and emerged with a 0 to 90 mph time of 22 seconds, and a consumption of 18 miles per gallon driven hard. Tanner also reported this coupé as having a single twin-choke downdraught Weber carburettor, single ignition and a standard four speed gearbox with synchromesh on third and top only. The specification of this model at the time led one to believe a fully synchromesh gearbox would be standard fitting, but since the A6GCS was

competing with a close-ratio gearbox with synchromesh on 3rd and top it may be that the factory installed this unit until experiments with the Porsche type fully synchromesh transmission were completed. The single ignition was certainly changed on the 1956 versions of the A6G/2000, and the single Weber was firstly changed for triple 36DO4s in 1955 and again altered in favour of three Weber 40DCO3s in 1957. It was, of course, possible for a customer in 1954 to request certain non-standard features for his Maserati, a courtesy extended by the factory and still applicable today.

Coachwork on the new production model was offered by Frua with his coupés and several lovely convertibles with varying grille treatments; Zagato offered a spider in 1954, a single example, and then concentrated on his low, lightweight coupés in 1955/56/57 by which time Allemano were completing several examples of their sombre looking berlina. The three carrozzeria Frua, Zagato and Allemano were the series builders of the A6G/2000 from 1954 to mid-1957 and between them offered a permutation of styles suited to most automobile tastes of the period.

The competition aspect was never far away even for the production models, and although not a road car in its strictest sense, the berlinetta offered by Pinin Farina and exhibited at the Turin Show in 1954 was an interesting study in what could have been available from this coachbuilder if his output had not been committed to the Ferrari 250GT. The two-tone blue berlinetta was certainly one of the meanest looking coupés ever put on a Maserati chassis, and was reputedly used for some determined road racing in Italy. I think the Show car was on chassis 2060 while its sister car was constructed on chassis 2059, which had already been driven on the Giro de Sicilia (Tour of Sicily) in April 1954. The third berlinetta was on chassis 2089 which originally was a sports racing A6GCS supplied to Francesco Giardini who had an accident with the car and subsequently sold it to Gianfranco Carisdeo. Through Sig. Dei in Rome another coupé was built by Pinin Farina, and returned to the owner who was resident at Ancona, on the Adriatic coast. The fourth coupé was number 2086 which again had a suspect history. Originally it was an A6GCS, number 2074, (which was never built by Maserati) and reallocated 2086. Pinin Farina clothed this berlinetta in May 1954 to the order of Sig. Palmieri. Thus all four berlinettas were built on the sports racing chassis and not on A6G/2000 chassis, although this equally could have been possible with a little 'stretching' of the aluminium and tubing. I was of the opinion that Frua attempted a berlinetta in 1955 but further research into factory archives revealed this was a coupé on the production chassis number 2063, with wet sump engine.

Several owners of the A6G/2000 Zagato coupé considered them an ideal Maserati with which to go road racing, certainly more competitive than either the Allemano or Frua versions. The gran turismo class of the 1956 Italian championship was won by Zagato 2-litre Maserati coupés, finally beating the Zagato 8V Fiats which were successful in 1954 and 1955. The combination of Stirling Moss and Denis Jenkinson used a Zagato coupé for a familiarization tour of the Mille Miglia circuit in preparation of their 1956 entry with a factory Tipo 350S. The car they used had already completed seven laps of this tortuous circuit before Moss got behind the wheel. So after 7000 tough miles it is worth noting that both Moss and 'Jenks' gave the model high marks. With Moss driving they agreed the coupé was extremely manouverable with light steering, visibility was good even in low seating and behind a narrow front screen and road adhesion was exemplary. I wonder if Moss really restricted himself to 6000 rpm.

The Zagato coupés were certainly faster than the Frua equivalent, the Perspex windows, basic interior trim and all aluminium coachwork contributed greatly to the minimal weight plus its low build and aerodynamic shape. The coachbuilder himself suggested his coupés could attain a top speed of 130 mph as opposed to the Frua version's 118 mph.

The A6G/2000 was built only in left hand drive form, and the cost in 1957 of the Zagato coupé was 8900 US dollars while the spider from Frua was the most expensive production 2-litre at 10,450 US dollars. Sales of this model seems to have been high in America where it was well received, possibly in the wake of competition success from the A6GCS. The handful of American importers reported, at the time, few problems with servicing and spare parts and it is likely that the factory placed the appropriate emphasis on after-sales service. No examples came to the UK, but several were sold in France, Belgium, Switzerland, South America and the home market, Italy.

The year 1957 was the final production period for the A6G/2000 which by now had received several improvements. Certainly twin ignition, twelve spark plugs, and triple Weber 40DCO3 carburettors were fitted on these late series engines although no revised bhp figures were issued by the factory. An unknown American motoring magazine (of 1957) published a journalist's impressions while at the wheel of an Allemano coupé, and that gearbox anomaly again became an issue. The road tester had difficulty in effecting smooth gearchanges, exactly the opposite of what Moss had said on his Mille Miglia test, and during conversation with a factory racing mechanic was told that although the specification led one to believe synchromesh gears were used the transmission had straight cut gears and no synchromesh. It may have been a case of 'you pays your money

and has what is available from the stores.' Fuel consumption was recorded at 13 mpg, a drastic increase over Tanner's original test in 1954; was this attributable purely to the weight of an Allemano coupé?

One of the nicest stories I have read about a 2-litre was reported by *Motor Trend* magazine in 1974. In a letter from a Mr R. C. Nicholson, a former owner of a twin-ignition Frua convertible, Fangio is reported to have located his car the night before the 1957 Sebring 12-hour race and asked if he could drive it. Fangio drove it down the Florida highway and unable to turn around put the car through a 360° turn. Mrs Nicholson was sitting beside the champion and he kissed her hand while travelling at well over 100 mph. His only reported comment was 'good brakes'. However, Nicholson said that it was a wild, hard-riding race car which had to be pointed like a rifle!

A6/1500, A6G/2000, A6GCS Berlinetta production

A6/1500	Pinin Farina	1946	051 052	2 cars
	coupés	1947	053 054 055	3 cars
		1948	056 057 058 059 060 061 062 063 064	9 cars
		1949	065 066 067 068 069 070 071 073 074 075 077 078 080 081 082 083 084 085 086 087 088 089 090	23 cars
		1950	072 079 091 092 095 076 093 094 098 096 097 099 0100 0101 0102 0103 0104 0105 0106 0107 0108 0109 0110	23 cars
A6G/2000 (single cam)	Vignale coupé	1951	2021	1 car
	Frua coupé	1951	2028	1 car
	Pinin Farina coupés and Frua cabriolets	1951/3	2013 2015 2017 2018 2020	9 cars
			2022 2023 2024 2025 2026 2027 2029 2030 2031	5 cars
A6G/2000 (twin cam)	Zagato spider	1954	2101	1 car
	Zagato coupés	1955	2102 2105 2106 2107 2112 2113	6 cars
		1956	2118 2121 2122 2123 2124 2137 2138 2148 2150 2155 2160 2179 2186 2189	14 cars
	Frua coupés	1955	2103 2114	2 cars
	Frua spiders	1955	2109	1 car
	Frua coupés/spiders	1956	2140 2180 2187 2181 2182	5 cars
	Frua coupés/spiders	1957	2183 2197 2191 2193 2192 2194 2196 2104 2110	9 cars
	Allemano coupés	1955	2108 2111	2 cars
		1956	2116 2117 2119 2120 2125 2142 2115 2126 2144 2165 2175 2146 2170 2184 2185	15 cars
		1957	2188 2190 2195 2198	4 cars
A6GCS Berlinetta	Pinin Farina	1954	2059 2060 2086	3 cars
		1955	2089	1 car
			TOTAL	**139 cars**

Factory records do not show the division of coupés to spiders by Frua for his A6G/2000 in 1955/56/57, but further research has shown a minimum of 9 open cars were made in total.

The 1947 A6/1500 Pinin Farina coupé with mechanically operated eyes

Complete with sunroof this was the model shown at the Geneva exhibition in 1947

Frontal treatment of what was reputedly the first postwar AG/1500. This photograph is from factory archives and bears the date 8 March 1946

It has a similarity to the cycle wing A6GCS; perhaps Orsi had ideas about a civilised sports car but where do you put the hardtop?

24

The hinged sunroof merely created a draught and was an impractical fitting which was not used again

The bonnet opening was lever operated from beneath the dash panel, and could open from either the exhaust or carburettor side. This useful feature remained on Pinin Farina coupés until late 1949

Ready for 1947 delivery, this coupé has headlights of conventional styling and shiny chrome Maserati hubcaps have become standard

Different wheel trims, no sunroof, and the petrol tank filler was inside the boot! On *Prova* plates ready for a run around the town in 1947

'Clean looking front but still fairly unexciting'. At least one version had horizontal air intakes between headlamps and the grille. The radiator roller blind was another standard feature

The 1947 1500 cc engine is here installed in a chassis prior to delivery to Carrozzeria Pinin Farina. The cam cover was always crackle-black finish. The location of the battery to fuel pump and single Weber carburettor might have been exciting!

26

Looking like an Italian taxi! The rear end view of a 1949 coupé

28

This cabriolet from Pinin Farina in 1948 was probably as much fun as the ladies seem to think. But what can the female in the middle be sitting on?

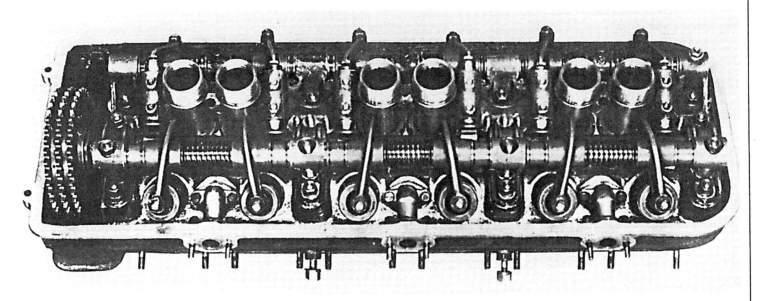

The cylinder head from an A6/1500 engine showing the triple-row sprocket for the single camshaft drive, and very long rocker arms

A slightly more attractive version with lower roofline and sharply inclined rear

The interior of the cabriolet shows individual front seats and minimum rear space. The instruments were white faced with the Trident motif on each; the clock was always recessed in glove comparment lid

29

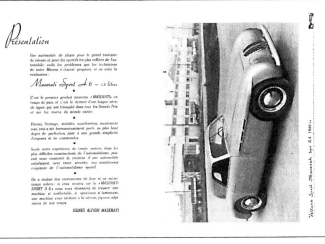

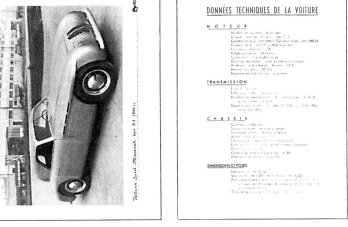

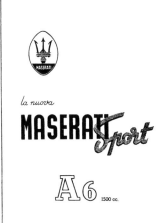

The first brochure was published in French for the 1947 Geneva Show. The 'sport' A6/1500 had its first public showing there. A photographic print of the car was stuck along one edge into the brochure.

Almost as an afterthought a similar single sheet sales leaflet was made available in the Italian language

Right and next page This 1949 brochure was the factory's first to use colour. Here the A6 coupé and cabriolet by Pinin Farina are linked with the sport aspect of the factory's activities with the A6GCS and Tipo 4CLT

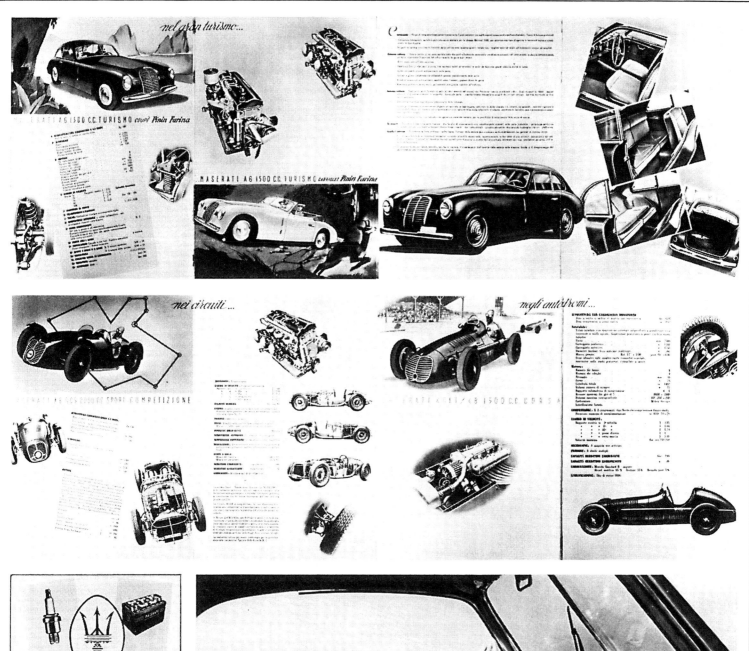

The 1951 single cam A6G/2000 coupé from Pinin Farina.
This was probably one of the first produced of 2-litre capacity
during the year. Upholstery is cord

Another style, somewhat
overweight, from the same
coachbuilder, Pinin Farina

The wire wheels help the
appearance of this coupé and
the overall height has been
reduced

This one is a little more rakish, and those silly sausage-like air vents have disappeared. This is chassis number 2020, a single cam 2-litre

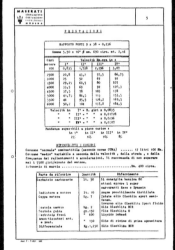

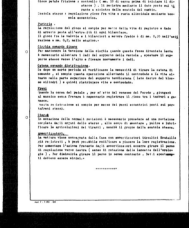

A nine page instruction manual was all the owner of an A6G/2000 found in the glovebox. This manual relates to a 1948 2-litre developing 100 bhp

The 'lira grin' by Vignale on chassis number 2021

36

2-litres ready for the 1951 Paris Show. *Left*, that lovely, single
cam Vignale coupé—the only one built; *centre*, a first series
Frua convertible and looking almost like a station wagon,
Pinin Farina's saloon to the *right*

The twin cam, single ignition
Frua coupé on chassis 2103,
built in 1955

Ready for the 1954 Turin Show, this is a 2-litre from Frua. Boot opening is by lever from inside the car. Rear end treatment is typical Frua with clean lines and quality fittings kept to a minimum

Frua's grille, on the other hand, is grotesque

On show at last! The 1954 Turin Show Frua A6G/2000
alongside the two-tone, competition berlinetta Maserati

The theme continues with this attractive convertible from
Frua on chassis number 2029 (single ignition)

A middle series A6G/2000 Frua spider. The exhaust system is
identical to the A6GCS

An artist's impression of
what the last 2-litre Frua
spider should look like for
1957. Maserati never
made up its mind—was it
to be spider or spyder?
Strictly it should be spider
for there is no 'y' in their
alphabet

40

With the hood erect this spider (which must have been by
Frua) certainly had a lovely line, and the coachbuilder
somehow managed to make the car appear taut and stubby

Another show model highlighting the Frua line with high wheel arches; these spiders were most attractive

The real thing on chassis number 2196—the wing mirrors are an unnecessary addition

Doing the 'just jobs' on a 2-litre at the factory in 1956

A completed rolling chassis, in this instance, a single ignition
car with the distributor drive off the rear of the inlet camshaft,
but fitted with the ultimate in Weber equipment of the time

A strange permutation! The coachwork is Frua, the bonnet
spring coils are a clue, but the engine is an A6GCS with the
oil filler nestling between the triple carburettors. Could it have
been a wet sump 2-litre with sports-racing cylinder head?

(*Right*) The successful Tipo 150S displayed on the Maserati
stand at the 1955 Paris Show. Alongside are an Allemano
berlina (*centre*) and Zagato coupé (*left*) both on the
A6G/2000 chassis

This is the slab-sided spider by Zagato on chassis number
2101 built in 1954

This is a single ignition, 2-litre in a Zagato coupé—not the
most powerful combination with those dreary 36DO4
carburettors

49

The interior of an A6G/2000 Zagato coupé was finished with
only the very basic equipment

50

The same Zagato spider is here exhibited at Geneva in 1955.
The nose treatment was eventually modified by the original
coachbuilder prior to this car being exported to the Argentine

As the car is today nestling in the USA with
converted grille

51

Above and right During the mid-nineteen fifties the Maserati company produced their own book entitled *Vittorie Maserati 1926–1954*. By today's standards it is antiquated but at the time it must have been very impressive. Although mostly about the company's success on the track it does, however, give some interesting comment on the factory itself and the production cars. Copies of these books are now highly valued

Roma

La Maserati nel mondo

New York

The dashboard with 'double eyebrows' by Zagato shows off a
more civilised steering wheel

Centre bonnet rib, accentuated grille, white roof line and electric aerial! A very shiny 1955 A6G/2000 Zagato coupé with everything

Stylised grille treatment by Zagato accompanies a very non-Zagato front bumper

The spare wheel of the Zagato coupés was secured by a three piece leather strap. Rear seating was non-existent, which kept the weight down!

Another version being used for what it was intended

Turckheim-Trois-Epis - 1956

A Zagato coupé at work in 1956

The same car. Front and rear bumpers appear interchangeable!

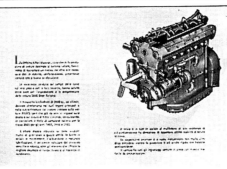

MASERATI "2000" GRAN TURISMO

Produced in February 1956, this brochure showed a more serious approach by the publicity staff to the Maserati production cars. The cabriolet by Frua is a first-series version. Its opposite number, the berlina, has a one-off Perspex fly catcher!

CABRIOLET A 6 G 2000/A

BERLINA A 6 G 2000/B

BERLINA A 6 G 2000/C

BERLINA A 6 G 2000/B

MASERATI GRAN TURISMO A 6 G 2000/C

Maserati's simple brochure for the early Allemano bodied 2-litre shows the car with a centre rib on the bonnet, a coachwork frill also done by Zagato

Zagato's 'double bubble' coupé on chassis number 2121 was
a one-off

Chassis number 2123; a
1956 Zagato coupé on its
roof in Austria

A Zagato coupé still competing in 1960 at a Swiss hillclimb
venue

Instead of repairing the
coachwork, this coupé was
converted. A mixture of
XKSS and 200SI

Whichever way you look at
this conversion, it's very ugly

62

1955 Paris Show; yet another grille treatment by Allemano
with his berlina

Geneva Show 1957 and the Allemano coupé has grown a
grille on the bonnet. It still did not have the appeal of a 2-litre
from Frua or Zagato

Allemano was the quantity
coachbuilder on the 2-litre
chassis

A 1956 version chassis 2115 now lives in Switzerland

The third berlinetta, chassis 2089, to be completed in 1955;
this version has angled louvres in the rear Plexiglass, but no
large fuel filler cap. The side air vents hint of Frua although it
has been confirmed this is the last road-going A6GCS by
Pinin Farina

The rear end, and that bumper are certainly Frua! Is the flap above the boot lid for fuel or oil for the dry sump system?

Complete with the Maserati distributor's name, Guglielmo Dei of Roma, it is likely this is the berlinetta which competed on the 1954 Tour of Sicily

Reputedly the berlinetta which found its way to the Paris distributor Thepenier. Bold white nose-to-tail stripe, Plexiglass bug-deflector; a most beautiful Maserati

66

A failing wheel bearing? The rear window had no louvres

Pure A6GCS was what the Pinin Farina berlinettas were
constructed on. Difficult to get into, difficult to get out of and
very noisy for the driver once on the move!

68

1954 Turin Show; this
berlinetta has a centre rib in
the windscreen and no air
scoop on the bonnet

Chassis 2059 as it is today
back in Italy. Apart from the
addition of an air vent near
the driver's door, and a
Formula 2 A6GCM *motore*,
this lovely Maserati is
original and still being used
in certain competitive events

MASERATI MODENA	CARATTERISTICHE DELL'AUTOTELAIO TIPO A6G2000		CILINDRATA 2000	V. CONTROLLO	DATA 29-1-58
	MOTORE N. 2183 - 166 TELAIO N. 2183				

MOTORE -

Testa cilindri *norm. A6G2000.*

Albero distribuzione *44126.*   Bilancieri *2 Piattelli prodotti ecc.*

Molle esterne per valvole *2 molle*   Molle interne *Carico 22kg.*

Valvole aspirazione *Ø42*   Valvole scarico *Ø38*

Ingranaggio distribuzione *tutti normali ecc. A6G2000*

Basamento cilindri *nr. A6G2000*

Canne cilindri *Bragonzi Ghisa Ø86.5*

Pistoni *Borgel tagliati* Volume camera scoppio in cm.² *RC 1:8,10*

Bielle *A6G2000*   Albero Motore *KMV. nr. A6G2000*

Bronzine di banco *e bielle normali Vanderwell*

Magnete o spinterogene *Marelli ST111 DTEM ant 10°*

Motorino *Marelli MT 23B.*   Dinamo *Marelli DN2A.*

Candele *Lodge RL4R.*   Carburatore *3 Weber 40DCO3*

Regolazione *Benzina*   Getto *120*   Diffusore *32*

Caratteristiche speciali *Gm.0,55 - Gp.0,55 - VF.125 - Segmenti v.b. Colette e asp. a ricircolazione d'acqua - Candele in bronzo con gommino - Alb. vsto fori entrata acqua al basamento - Modifica tendicatena - Anqvs alb motore.*

RIZIONE (x) Disco *1 A6G2000*   Molle *A6G2000*   Spingidisco *A6G2000*

Leve di comando *tutto normale tipo elastico con 2 dischi incollati al in cuscio. RV2*

Fase *AA33 - AB65)0.30 / CA62 - CS25)*

AMBIO - Scatola *A6G2000*

Rapporti: Iº *12/30*   IIº *19/23*   IIIº *22/20*   IVº *25/12*
tutte sincronizzate

Pompa olio *solo mandata con modifica valvo b A6G2000.*

PONTE POSTERIORE - Rapporto *9/40*   Albero di trasmissione *Fabbri Ø80*

Mozzi *norm. Altri vedi A6GCS* Ammortizzatori *A6G2000*

Molle *2 a balestra norm. A6G2000*

AVANTRENO - Mozzi *A6GCS.*   Ammortizzatori *A6G2000*

Molle *2 a spirale 1° tipo con scodellini di compensazione Ø14*

STERZO - Comandi *A6GCS*   Snodi *a sfera ecc.*
Piantone 2 Fabbri Ø48

FRENI - Diametro m/m *328x60 - 290x50*   Tamburi *A6GCS*

Ceppi *A6GCS*   Portafreni *A6GCS*

Pompe *Ant Ø1"1/4 - post 1" con mento. Frendo 553 - Freno a mano sulla trasmiss.*

TELAIO - Caratteristiche speciali *Costruito da Gilco*

Radiatore *A6G2000*   Serbatoio carburante *80l. Fian*

Pompa benzina *Elettrica Fispa*

Batterie accumulatori *Hensemberger. 12V.*

Bobina *2 Marelli, SB11 DTEM* Impianto elettrico *12V.*

Ruote *a Raggi Borrani*   Gomme *Pirelli Stelv. ant 600 16 - post 600 16   x 1 Cabriolet. 2x - Frizione non elastica - Ventilatore ultimot.*

NOTE: *1x Berlina 2-4 posti - FRUA - Tapezzeria Cajote nera Strumenti Jaeg. in Inglese con Contamiglia - Fari C.b.c - antinebb. C. Apparecchio Riscald. Smiths - Marmitta Abarth Verniciata avorio con fasua sl. colmo Mon-*

69

The standard build sheet completed by the factory for each car, in this case an A6G/2000 of 1957. Chassis/engine number 2183 shows this to be a twin ignition 2-litre with triple Weber 40DCO3 carburettors. This model was never a berlina but a spider by Frua. The chassis was by Gilco while the 80-litre fuel tank was from Fiandri who made many of the sports racing A6GCS bodies. This particular Maserati is now owned by John Duggleby and is the only example in the UK.

70

PART·2

The 3500 series—1957 to 1970

The A6G/2000 models were continued throughout most of 1957, the last year of its production. However, during 1956, Ing. Giulio Alfieri now chief design engineer had begun work on a production 3·5-litre engine 'in theory' based on the six cylinder Tipo 350S credited to Ing. Bellentani. His brief from Orsi was to develop a unit (without any of the aggravations of a racing engine) which could go into a production chassis for sale to the public. The heritage of this new motor lay with the 350S which in turn was more related to the A6G/2000 than its direct predecessor, the sports racing 300S. Ing. Alfieri dispensed with the screw-type tappet adjusters, his reason being that this system had a high degree of wear through inadequate lubrication and was not, therefore, suitable for a reliable road car. He adopted the piston-(or bucket-) type tappets with shims for clearance adjustments. The twin camshafts were chain driven, a spur gear connecting the lower sprocket to the crankshaft. Ignition for the twelve spark plugs came from one Marelli ST111 distributor, flange-mounted on the left hand side of the engine. This distributor used twin contact points and an offset rotor, with twin Marelli coils mounted on the engine bulkhead. Carburation was to be by triple 42DCOE3 Webers through a large oval air cleaner with sausage Fiamm element inside.

Lubrication on these early production engines appears to have been a compromise between the 350S and some new thinking by Alfieri. He initially retained the external pipes circulating oil under pressure through a horizontally mounted filter beneath the carburettors. Changing the oil filter element was not an easy chore! The dry sump system disappeared together with the scavenge pump, and a large finned wet sump was introduced. An all synchromesh four-speed gearbox from ZF was mated to a ten inch Borg and Beck clutch. A Salisbury rear axle with a choice of seven optional ratios, Girling braking system, Boranni disc type wheels with aluminium rims, ZF steering box, Hardy Spicer prop shaft and couplings, Alford and Alder suspension were all used. It would seem that Orsi had some international connections, and it makes one realize that Ing. Alfieri did most of the work!

The prototype 3500GT was shown at Geneva on 20 March 1957, and in this form the engine gave 226 bhp at 5500 rpm. Coachwork was a Touring of Milan *superleggera* (extra light) all aluminium 2-door coupé. At the same time Allemano created his own design for the 3·5 litre, 3500/A, or Maserati GT di Lusso 3500/T for the *superleggera* version.

In February 1968 the factory let you know that you'd arrived!

71

By the time the Turin Show of 1957 arrived, Alfieri had redesigned the camshafts and some small details for the engine to now realize 230 bhp. The 3500GT coupé was well received by motoring press, the products' distributors and potential customers. Orders for the initial production came mainly from the home country, the Italians certainly liking this brutal coupé.

The first 3500 exported to America, where Orsi had hoped his volume sales would be, was tested by *Sports Car Illustrated* magazine in November 1958. The price was 11,400 US dollars through the distributor Maserati Corporation of America, on Long Island. The magazine testers attained a maximum with the coupé of 130 mph, a standing quarter mile time of 16·8 seconds and returned a fuel consumption of 15 mpg. They reported that although driving position and seating was comfortable, the ride was choppy and fast cornering would readily induce the rear end to drift out. Motoring hard in the wet was never recommended in the coupé anyway.

During late 1959 Ing. Alfieri returned to the design office and virtually redesigned the complete six cylinder engine to give greater flexibility, smoothness and for his mentor, a lower production-to-sales-cost ratio. The carburettors were changed to 42DCOE6s, the cylinder head featured new water passages, compression was 8·5 to 1 and the four-ring Borgo pistons had lower cutaway skirts to clear the crankshaft counterweights. Power was now up to 260 bhp (230 CUNA standards). Production of the new model was about 100 in 1959 but by 1960, manufacture and distribution of the coupés had become organized. Touring of Milan was the exclusive bodybuilder as Allemano had decided to rest.

Front disc brakes with vacuum-operated servo were a standard fitting in 1960, those substantial aluminium finned drums could cope no longer with the power and weight of the car. The transmission was changed for 1961 into five speeds, although if a customer had the particular desire, the four-speed transmission could be retained. *Car and Driver* magazine tried one of the late 1960 models in the summer of 1961 and criticised the power under 3000 rpm, arguing that it was not as smooth as the 1959 version. Their test car had front discs, but the four-speed gearbox, which incidentally was the same unit as fitted to the BMW 507. Fuel consumption had moved down drastically to 13 mpg, but it was possible the test car was incorrectly jetted.

In 1961, the Vignale spider became available and the 4 inch shorter wheelbase made a great improvement to roadholding, although everyone complained about the ground clearance, which was less than its regular 5 inches at the point where the exhaust located beneath the chassis cross-member. These first production convertibles were fitted with four-speed transmissions although Vignale kindly gave his customers electric windows! Price of the spider was 12,300 US dollars.

For 1962 disc brakes were the first improvement, and they were certainly now required as the 3500 engine had undergone further detail changes resulting in a few more horse power. Lucas fuel injection was fitted to the six cylinder unit (hence GTI, or *inezione*), although a customer could specify carburettors for his car in advance. Carrozzeria Touring had detailed his coachwork inside and out, wire wheels were popular but not standard although by now electric windows and aerial were. Factory production was up to almost ten cars per week compared with eight a week in 1960. These figures included the convertibles and, introduced in 1962, Vignale's coupé, the Sebring.

The UK importers loaned a 3500 version of the Sebring, registration 41 GUC, to *Autocar* in late 1963. The road testers were enthusiastic about the Vignale coupé suggesting it had poise and balanced proportions. Their model was, of course, right-hand drive, had wire wheels and American air conditioning/refrigeration. *Autocar* staff obviously had a fine time with this £5000-plus car, driving in excess of 1000 miles averaging, 14·8 mpg and using three pints of oil. Top speed was 137 mph and the standing quarter remained at 16 seconds. In 1963, the UK price of the Maserati Sebring kept it fairly exclusive and as a result not a great number were imported. Since this was also the case in America, not being as popular as the 3500 Touring coupés, the factory found sales elsewhere in Europe and in Australia.

The 1964 Turin Show saw the exhibition of an eventual replacement for the 3500 coupé. Designed by Frua, built by Maggiora of Turin, the Mistral was certainly destined to become one of Maserati's profitable models. It was to enjoy a long production life, 1963 to 1970, a total of 828 coupés and 120 spiders being finished, which is an average of almost three per week. One must remember that the Sebring was also being produced and that the series II Sebring came during 1965, so it was a flourishing period at Modena.

The Mistral was steel bodied with the exception of doors, bonnet and rear opening panel being in aluminium. *Road & Track* tested a 4-litre spider in 1968 loaned by Bob Grossman, a US Maserati distributor and sometime Ferrari driver. This magazine accorded high marks for reliability, quality and appearance although considered the Mistral coupé better looking. At last, however, someone noted the flexibility of this six cylinder engine which was certainly able to crawl up a hill in fifth gear without fuss using only 1500 rpm. The convertible was selling in the USA for almost 15,000 US dollars which obviously placed it alongside certain Ferraris and other exotic automobiles; Orsi had a tough nut to crack. However, while this model was not without customers from the UK and Europe it never peaked in America and aside from the 3500 in 1960, Maserati had so far made no great sales impact into this lucrative automobile market.

At the time Tony Hogg (of *Road & Track*) made an observation about Maserati which many feel is true even today. He said 'In the last decade, the Maserati trident has been largely overshadowed by the Ferrari prancing horse. This situation has come about through financial trouble at Maserati combined with the very comprehensive and successful racing programme pursued by Ferrari'. It was true in 1968 for certain.

Up to 1970, the last year of the front-engined straight sixes, it was clear that Maserati had made available much optional equipment. It could never be categorically stated that a specific model had come off the production line with what was actually current at the time. The factory, through its distributors, were always able to tailor a model to a customer's requirements. For example, they may have exhibited a wire wheel, five speed 3500 at some motor show announcing it as a new model, and for some months after they would continue producing the previous version. Individual in their outlook and practises, was Orsi operating the factory profitably?

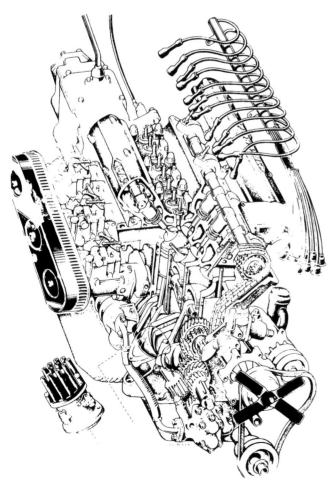

3500GT production

3500GT	Allemano coupés	1958	3 cars
		1959	1 car
3500GT	Bertone coupé	1959	1 car
3500GT/GTI	Frua spider	1959	1 car
	Touring of Milan coupés	1957	2 cars
		1958	119 cars
		1959	195 cars
		1960	366 cars
		1961	448 cars
		1962	390 cars
		1963	399 cars
		1964	55 cars
		1965	1 car
	Vignale spiders	1959	2 cars
		1960	88 cars
		1961	79 cars
		1962	47 cars
		1963	21 cars
		1964	5 cars
Sebring series I	Vignale coupés	1962	49 cars
		1963	203 cars
		1964	92 cars
		1965	4 cars
Sebring series II	Vignale coupés	1965	86 cars
		1966	12 cars
Mistral	Frua coupés	1963	1 car
		1964	99 cars
		1965	177 cars
		1966	218 cars
		1967	199 cars
		1968	109 cars
		1969	23 cars
		1970	2 cars
Mistral	Frua spiders	1964	17 cars
		1965	31 cars
		1966	29 cars
		1967	24 cars
		1968	12 cars
		1969	6 cars
		1970	1 car
		TOTAL	3617 cars

This cutaway drawing was issued in postcard form by J. Thepenier presumably to potential buyers of the 3500. It does, however, show the blanked-off water outlets between the cylinder head nuts suggesting that the very early models were still utilising the head castings of the 350S

The factory jig-built 3500 chassis was a simple affair. The main centre tubing was oval, supplied by one of Orsi's outside manufacturing companies

74

Then came the welded steel panel supports for the critical areas, and the car begins to look like a truck!

The first series 3500 engine with that horizontally mounted oil filter visible beneath the air filter casing

A 1958 3·5-litre engine with triple Weber carburettors

An early Touring of Milan coupé with the poor drum brakes, although servo assisted, and that funny cranked gearlever for the four-speed transmission

77

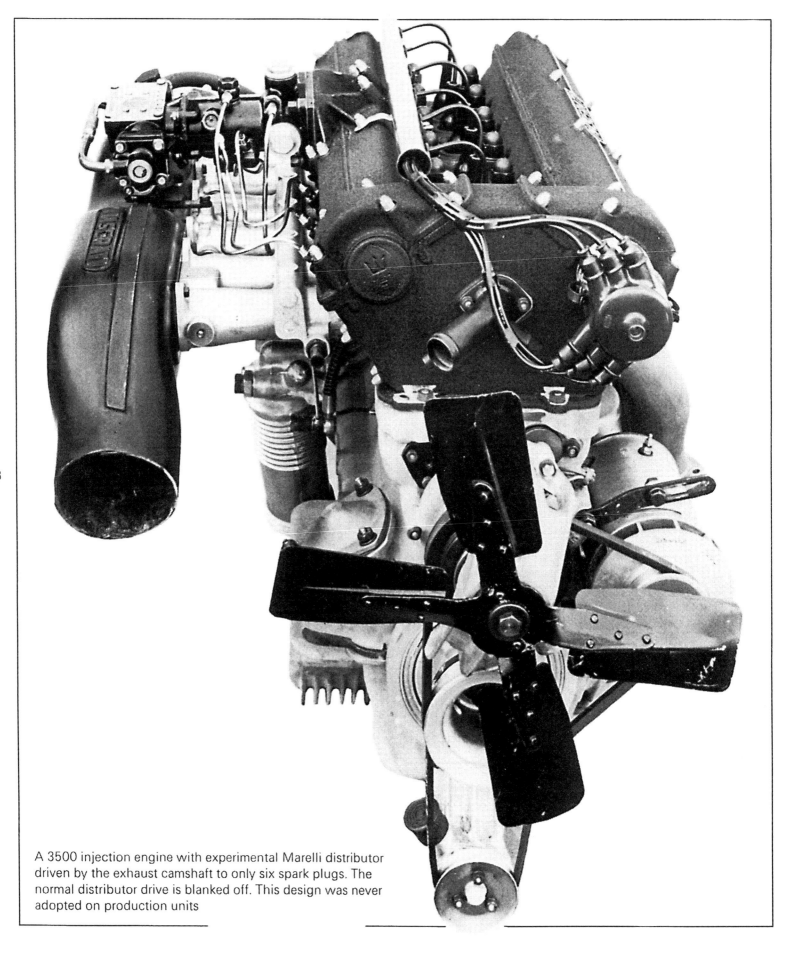

A 3500 injection engine with experimental Marelli distributor driven by the exhaust camshaft to only six spark plugs. The normal distributor drive is blanked off. This design was never adopted on production units

Clean looking 12-plug engine! This is also a 1958 edition
with the cam chain tensioner just above the dynamo

The prototype 3500, chassis number 001, on the scrapheap
in 1971. Wonder how far it actually travelled?

The first 3500GT outside the factory in 1957 with 'painted'
Pirelli Stelvio tyres and rear window wiper

The Allemano version of the 3500GT was in short supply,
this coachbuilder not having the output equivalent to Touring
of Milan

Side indicators on the roof line, twin radio aerials and very
spacious luggage accommodation; 1957 Allemano version

Strangely Allemano did the electric window gadgetry first on the 3500. And that very individual gearlever

Presumably all you required for a weekend. Touring of Milan 1957 model

An early 3500 in a Modena street on English licence plates.
The well-dressed gentleman is American journalist Peter Coltrin

One of the first 1958 production coupés was sold to Switzerland where it stayed until 1972. This model had the instruments of a 2-litre model

1958 version by Touring of Milan. The white-knobbed gearlever signifies four speeds; note the wind-up windows

The spare wheel was stowed beneath the boot floor. Quilted
stick-on plastic was normal on the Touring of Milan cars for
1957/58/59

The completed car on Milan licence plates. No side quarter glass, no external frills but a handsome model

The factory doing their public relations act for the 1957 Paris Salon

Stirling Moss about to chauffeur Bertocchi in a series I
3500GT with some expensive wire wheels fitted

This 3·5 litre by Bertone was exhibited at the 1959 Turin Show. The rear end is a massacre of metal!

Frua tried hard with the 3500 in convertible form, but it became overloaded with flash fittings

It looked better with the hood erect, although nearly as much chrome littered the side panels. Only one car was made

Frua got it right with his 3·5 litre coupé. The wire wheel model had Sebring rear lights and came with a fuel injected engine

Frontal treatment influenced Frua thinking for the
Quattroporte design a year later

Subtle changes improve this other Frua bodied 3500,
although it still appears a large car

The rear end treatment was
similar to his wire wheel
version; maybe Frua tired of
designing boots!

Carrozzeria Boneschi of Milan titled this the Berlina 'Tight' 2
plus 2 on the 3500GT chassis and exhibited it at the 1962
Turin Show

Boneschi named this Geneva 1963 creation the same, but it
wasn't

The rear end was a failure with its razor edge construction.

The Touring of Milan coupé in its final form. Note twin quarter lights

The interior with round screw knob for opening quarter glass, electric window switches in the door panel, Maserati gear knob and smokers' dustbin for the rear passengers

The Lucas fuel injection installation on the 1962 3·5 litre. The rigid chrome plated injector pipes were later replaced with a Neoprene type material and the metering unit was redesigned to incorporate an oil pump

Hood up. A convertible by Touring of Milan which failed to please

Hood down. According to Hans Tanner, Carrozzeria Touring built five of these convertibles based on the series I 3500 chassis

A 1961 spider by Vignale which was never adopted by the factory. It is likely that two such designs were built on the 3500 chassis both with four-speed gearboxes

The back-end treatment did little to enhance this model
(Vignale 1961 3500 spider)

The fuel injection 3500 Vignale spider really was as good as it looked. The wire wheels with three-eared spinners were a costly extra

A careful look at these two Vignale spiders inside the factory compound during 1962, will show a different design for the hardtops

A 1964 3500GTI spider. Borrani disc wheels did not detract from this roadster's appeal

Ready for the bad weather! The twin silencers beneath the driver's door were standard with a third silencer mounted transversely under the rear bumper

Injection engine installation in a 1963 spider, number AM101:2751. Note the firing order stamped on the exhaust cam cover and substantial moulded air intake box beneath the metering unit

A Vignale advertisement from *Quattroroute* of November 1964

101

Wood veneer dashboard, electric windows, five speed gearbox. Vignale executed this one-off in the hope of attracting fresh orders for his coachworks

The real thing although looking somewhat like a Fiat Dino spider

A Maserati Sebring at the Geneva
Show. This is a first series model but
with strange rear lights

The Maserati importer for Germany, Auto-König, phasing out
the old and introducing the new. Two series I Sebrings
alongside a late 3500GTI in the showroom

A series II Sebring with
altered side air vent, air
scoops just ahead of
windscreen and different
headlamp arrangement

Interior of the car *below left* with fake air conditioning plant
above the switches

The interior of the early Sebring with plastic rocker switches
and imitation wood dash

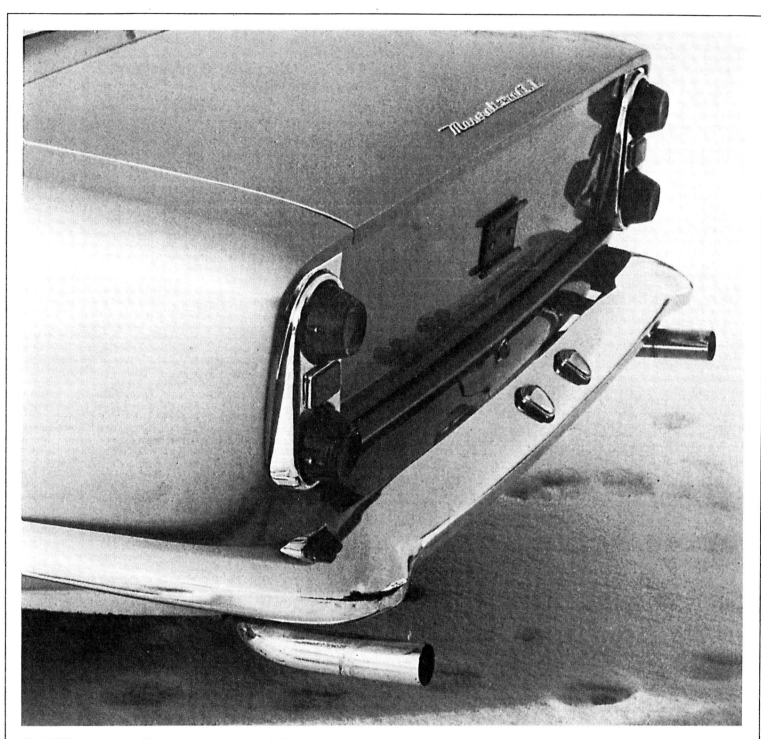

3500GTI Sebring by Vignale showing rear light treatment
identical to late series 3500 by Touring of Milan

The last development of the
Sebring. It is not just the wire
wheels that make it stand up,
somehow Vignale raised his
coachwork off the series II
chassis

Interior with revised centre
console and new position for
electric window switches
instead of in the door panel.
Air conditioning in this car is
real; the clock and cigar
lighter were standard items

macchine di classe
esigono
prodotti di classe

An advertisement from a 1966 *Quattroroute*. I assume plugging the virtues of Supercortemaggiore for high performance cars. Was the crash helmet really necessary with the Mistral spider?

109

A right hand drive version of the 3·7 litre Mistral with the optional wire wheels

Frua got the Mistral spider absolutely right, and made it one of the finest looking Maseratis ever produced in volume. This is a 1965 3700 cc version

A 4-litre Mistral coupé at the Geneva Show in early 1965

Mistral production line at the factory in 1967

A novel style of exhibiting your wares! This was how each model was delivered back to Maserati from Officine Padane (responsible only for glass, paint and trim having received bodyshells from Maggiora unfinished), ready for engine and running gear installation

Instrumentation in the Mistral was neat, the anodised-rim
gauges first appeared with the Sebring series II

Some owners never did get used to the injection system!
Here is a 3·7 engine with the metering unit (driven off the
inlet camshaft) blanked off and triple Webers installed
instead

The way it was when Ing. Alfieri designed it

The 4-litre Mistral coupé was a practical car that became
much in demand. This one has just sprinted the autostrada
into its home town of Modena

Some of the supposedly late series models had early features,
A 1967 Mistral spider with wind up windows instead of
electric

The hardtop by Frua did nothing to enhance the appearance

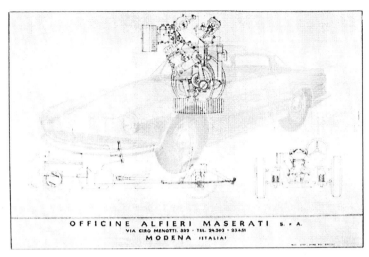

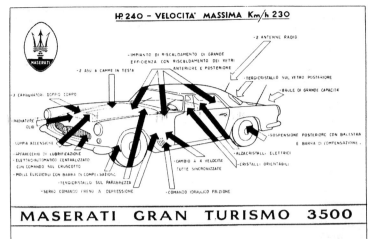

A rather handsome two-door coupé by Bertone is superimposed on the first brochure announcing the 3500GT in 1957. The hard sell is on the reverse

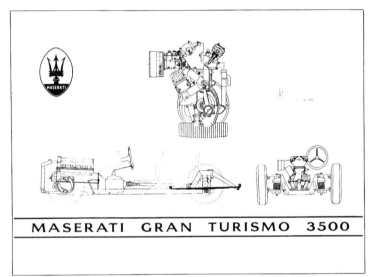

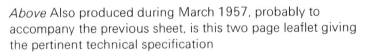

Above Also produced during March 1957, probably to accompany the previous sheet, is this two page leaflet giving the pertinent technical specification

Below The very first 3500GT by Touring of Milan, with those funny recessed side indicators, was the reason for yet another two page brochure, this time published in June 1957

Solidi imbottiti razionalmente, I sedili anteriori, regolabili e scorrevoli, anche a posizione arretrata, rendono facile l'accesso ai sedili posteriori.

Seats shaped for exceptional comfort. The front seats are adjustable and allow easy access to the back seats even in posterior position.

Sièges très confortables. Les sièges avant sont ajustables séparement. On y accède facilement aux sièges arrière en rabattant les sièges avant.

Posto di guida confortevole e grande luminosità e visibilità. Copertura del cruscotto in materiale antiriflesso.

Position du conducteur avec grande visibilité. Le tablier est en matériel antireflection.

Comfortable driving position, with exceptional visibility. Instrument panel covered by antireflection material.

Sospensione anteriore funzionante su gomma ed a giunto sferico.

Suspension avant fonctionnant sur caoutchouc et avec jointure sphérique.

Front suspension functions on rubber and with spherical joints.

Vista anteriore della vettura a cofano alzato che mette in evidenza il vano motore.

Vue avant de la voiture avec capote levée montrant le moteur.

Front view of the car with hood up showing the engine compartment.

Motore 6 cilindri, doppia accensione.

Moteur 6 cylindres double allumage.

The 6 cylinder engine has twin ignition.

Vista posteriore della vettura. La ruota di scorta disposta sotto il piano permette un completo utilizzo dello spazio per bagagli.

Vue arrière de la voiture. Roue de rechange dans un porte-roue qui permet l'usage complet du compartiment de bagages.

Rear view of the car. The spare wheel stored under the floor allows for ample luggage space.

A coloured brochure showing an early type 3500GT was the factory's next effort. It is interesting to note the absence of quarter-lights and in the engine compartment, no thermostat in the cooling system

The 3500GT always looked better in dark colours. Are they using the same model lady? This sales brochure makes the first mention of optional 'disk' brakes up front

MASERATI

GRAN TURISMO 3500

April 1960—this sales brochure gave us the first chance of disc brakes as standard equipment

An artist's impression of what could be a 2-litre car. This brochure, without colour or coloured illustrations, introduced fuel injection together with Vignale's convertible

121

Back to colour again. Vignale's lovely 'spyder' on the short wheelbase chassis graces the front page. This is an early model with carburettor engine and four speed transmission

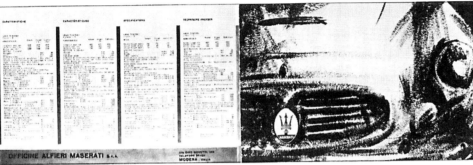

The same artist. Here comes the Vignale coupé S (or Sebring) on the same chassis as the spider

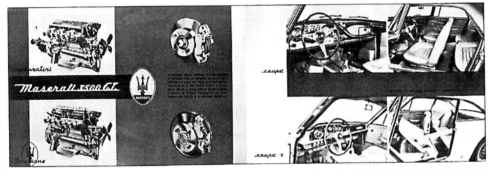

122

The Vignale Sebring could be purchased in 3500, 3700 and 4000 cc versions. This brochure was the first of a Maserati house style with specifications in English, French, German and Italian

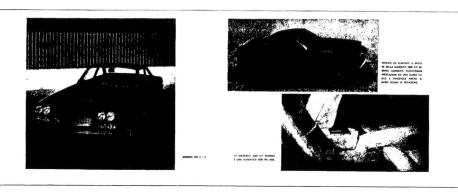

A wire wheel Sebring 2 + 2 brochure showing a series II car but informing us of the earlier 3485 cc engine. The English translation is nothing short of terrible

The quality of design of this sales brochure for the Mistral was exceptional; one can almost smell the leather interior. A wire wheel spider, in either 3·7 or 4-litre form, is nowadays considered a worthwhile investment

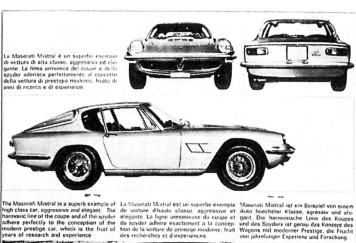

La Maserati Mistral è un superbo esempio di vettura di alta classe, aggressiva ed elegante. La linea armonica del coupe e della spyder aderisce perfettamente al concetto della vettura di prestigio moderna, frutto di anni di ricerca e di esperienza

The Maserati Mistral is a superb example of high class car, aggressive and elegant. The harmonic line of the coupe and of the spyder adhere perfectly to the conception of the modern prestige car, which is the fruit of years of research and experience.

La Maserati Mistral est un superbe exemple de voiture d'haute classe, aggressive et elegante. La ligne armonieuse du coupe et du Spyder adhere exactement à la conception de la voiture de prestige moderne, fruit des recherches et d'expériences.

Maserati Mistral ist ein Beispiel von einem Auto hoechster Klasse, agressiv und elegant. Die harmonische Linie des Koupes und des Spyders ist genau das Konzept des Wagens mit moderner Prestige, die Frucht von jahrelanger Experienz und Forschung.

I sedili sono il risultato di uno studio inteso a ridurre al minimo la fatica sui lunghi percorsi. Gli strumenti sono disposti nel cruscotto in modo funzionale ed efficiente. Il baule è di una ampiezza insolitamente grande per una vettura 2 posti.

The seats are the result of a study made to reduce fatigue to a minimum on long distances.
The instruments are functionally and efficiently located.
Unusual for a two seater, the boot has an extremely large capacity.

Les sièges sont le résultat d'un etude effectué pour réduire la fatigue au minimum
Les instruments sont placé avec rationalite dans le tableau de bord.
Insolit pour une voiture 2 places, le coffre a bagages a une grande capacite.

Die Sitze sind das Resultat intensiver Studien um die Müdigkeit auf langen Strecken zu reduzieren.
Die Strumente sind am Armaturenbrett in funzionaler und wirksamer Art angebracht.
Der Kofferraum ist besonders gross einen Zweisitzer.

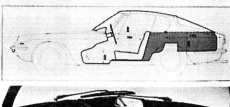

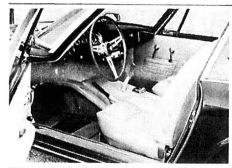

L'INTERNO

L'interno è funzionale ed armonioso, sia per la disposizione degli strumenti che per il disegno delle finiture fatica al minimo

The interior fittings of the car are of superb quality both in the materials used and in the design. The seats themselves are very comfortable being the result of concentrated research to reduce fatigue to a minimum

L'interieur est fonctionnel et harmonieux a la presentation generale. Les sièges resultent d'une etude speciale afin de reduire la fatigue au minimum

Das Innere ist funktionell und schön ausgestattet, sei es die Anordnung der Instrumente oder die vollkommene Ausführung der Einrichtungen. Die Sitze sind das Resultat eines intensiven Studiums und tragen dazu bei, Müdigkeitserscheinungen auf ein Minimum zu reduzieren

GLI STRUMENTI

Gli strumenti sono disposti nel cruscotto in modo da permettere la visibilità senza distrarre la guida.

The dashboard has all the instruments grouped in such a way that it is possible to read any one without detracting attention from the road ahead

Le tableau de bord groupe tous les instruments d'une façon telle qu'elle permet de les lire sans que le regard ne quitte jamais la route.

Die Instrumente sind so übersichtlich am Armaturenbrett angebracht, dass sie eine Handhabung erlauben ohne die Lenkung des Wagens zu beeinflussen

IL COUPE

Il coupé 2 posti è l'ultima concezione di alta classe e di eleganza. La visibilità è perfetta e contribuisce ad una guida facile e ad una grande sicurezza.

The two seater coupé is the ultimate concept of high performance and elegance. The visibility from inside is reassuring and contributes greatly to a superb driving position and fullest confidence.

Le coupé 2 places est l'ultime conception des performances elevees alliées à l'elegance. Le visibilite est parfaite et contribue grandement à une conduite aisée et à la pleine detente.

Das zweisitzige Coupe ist die letzte Zubildgung hoher Klasse und Eleganz. Die Sichtverhältnisse sind ausgezeichnet und sichern eine leichte Führung des Fahrzeugs und grosse Sicherheit.

The brochure gives us 'Mistral'. Some factory instruction manuals and the nameplate badge above the rear bumper give us 'Mistrale'. Whichever, the brochure and car are beautiful

MASERATI AUTOMOBILI MODENA | INSTRUCTION MANUAL FOR MASERATI 3500 G.T. | 1

P R E F A C E

In this booklet we have briefly gathered the main principles covering this car, together with informations for the knowledge and for the normal operations of use and maintenance of the car.
In order to obtain the bestresults from the car as far as minimum cost, long life and best performance are concerned, one should bear in mind the suggestions given in this book.
For those operations and repairs not easely done with normal tools at one's disposal (supplied with ordinary tool kit), as well for complete or partial overhauling, we suggest those Owners, in their own interest, to ovail themselves of the services of our Agents who will look to the prompt, accurate and rational execution of any yob of repair or overhauling.
All spare parts must be original for the best functionning resukts.
Engine and chassis numbers must be givenwhen ordering spares.

DATA FOR IDENTIFICATION OF A VEHICLE

Each car is identified by special nimbers, i. e. :

AM 101 ☆ . . . . ☆
AM 101 S ☆ . . . . ☆
AM 101 C ☆ . . . . ☆

The chassis serial number is stamped on the right hand side of the cross member and on both sides of this number appear the Maserati trade mark.
The engine number is stamped on the clucch housing near the starting motor.
These numbers, for easy reading, are repeated on two plaques mountedon the radiator shroud, and are the only ones suitable both for identificatio and sale of the car, they also appear on the certificate of origin and on the registration certificate.

MASERATI AUTOMOBILI MODENA | INSTRUCTION MANUAL FOR MASERATI 3500 G.T. | 2

SPECIFICATIONS

Number of cylinders	6 in line
Bore and stroke .....(3,38 x 3,93 inch)	86 x 100 mm.
Individual cyl. capacity (35,4 cu.inch)	580,88 cc.
Total capacity ..... (212 cu. inch) ...	4385,29 cc.
Max. power at 5800 revs/min. Injection	235 CV.
" " " " " " Carburettors	220 CV.
Taxable power	33 CV.

Cylinder block is of light alloy with liners of special cast iron.
Cylinder head is made of a light alloy with overhead valves, in which th valve seats have ben inserted.
Combustion chambers are hemispherical.
The crankshaft is dynamically balanced and is supported by seven lead-indium alloy bearings.
The conrods are made of forged steel in H section with the bigend bearing made of lead-indium alloy.
The little end bearing is a bronze bush.
Pistons are made of light alloy awith two compression rings and two oil rings.
Crankshaft has torsional damper.

DISTRIBUTION

The inclined valves in the head are actuated by 2 overhead camshafts driven by a 3 - cog chain.
Valves are operated direcly by the camshaft with the interposition of a small steel tappets operating in cast-iron seats.
Valve clearance is by means of casehardened steel inserts, which may be easily replaced.
The proper clearances (cold) between tappets and the base radius of the lobe of cam are 0,1 mm. inlet 0,21 mm exaust.
This will give the following data.
Lift of the inlet valve at top dead centre: 1 mm. (0,004)
lift of the ex. valve at top dead centre : 0,9mm. (0,039)

INTAKE COLLECTOR

The intake collector in a light alloy made, with water chamber for the warming up of the mixture.
In the hot season or in normaly hot areas, the water should not circulate inside the collector.
This is to improve the engine performance and make starting easier.

MASERATI AUTOMOBILI MODENA | INSTRUCTION MANUAL FOR MASERATI 3500 G.T. | 3

F U E L   F E E D I N G - INJECTION

The Feed is obtained by fuel being injected inside the intake collector, (Indirect injection).
This is achieved by a Lucas fuel pump, distributor, and a control unit.
The pump is electricaly driven and it is capable of compressing the petrol to a pressure of 7 atmospheres.
The pump performance is very satisfactory, absorbing 60 watts only, with a fuel flowing capacity of 130 liters/h. to a pressure of 7 kgs. per cm.^{2} (Squared contimeter).
The pressure brings the fuel to a unit which is called "the distributor".
This distributor distributes the pressure to the appropriate injector, causing it to open, permitting a very precise fuel metering into the cylinders, in exactly the amount required by the engine, according to the setting of the control instrument .
The distributor has the advantage of not employing heavy components with alternate motion, nor elastic or return adyustments, the little cylinders being operated by pressure.
Figure no. 1 shows the distributor scheme.
One can note how the motion of one rotor, bearing certain holes, connects the little cylinders alleys with the pressure and how the rotor itself, with a further rotation, connects the same amount of pressured petrol with the tubing which conveys the fuel to,the injector.
This system is particulary simple.
Also the control system, which determines the amount of fuel conveyed inside the intake ports according to the amount of air inspired by the cylinders, is very simple, as well as its adjustment.
The adjustment is effectuated by means of rollers or springs, the flexibility of which has a considerable importance.
Figure 2 shows the control scheme and particularly, at point A, B, C, the coupled rollers determining the variation of motion of the distributor cylinders.
Points D, E, show the springs which vary the rollers operating place, on the plane.
The position and influence of springs D, E, are particulerly important, since they determine the depressure capacity curve.
Rollers A, B, C, are only the elements providing the flowing c city amount.
The control element is also equipped with a fuel flowing varietor, the performance of which is given by the Barometric depressure.
Oil lubrication of the injection system is provided by a slightly higher pressure then fuel's.

MASERATI AUTOMOBILI MODENA | INSTRUCTION MANUAL FOR MASERATI 3500 G.T. | 4

The distributor element is equipped with a constant level pump, with a pressure adyusting valve, which prevent fuel escape throughout the rotating components.

S T A R T E R

In the winter season an easier starting of the cold engine is obtained by an additional aumont of injected petrol and air which helps winning the cold engine friction, and permits the engine normal idling in the cold season as well.
This additional amount of air and petrol is obtained by operating a dashboard switch (choke) which can increase the mixture to three times the normal amount.
It is up to the driver to gradualy reduce this feed enreachment, setting the switch bach to zero position, as soon as the engine is perfectly hot.

SAFETY SWITCH

If the engine does not come into life when setting the starting key on, a safety system causes the authomatic diconnection of the fuel feeding pump and, contemporaneously, a red warning light lights up on the dashboard.
the safety system is operated also when the engine oil pressure cut down beneath the 0,5 kgs. per cm^2 (squared centimeter).
To resed the pump into action, push the warning light button.
An additional switch, situated under the dashoard, eliminates the safety system efficiency, should this become defectable, and connects the pump directly with the ignition switch.

MASERATI AUTOMOBILI MODENA | Distributore "LUCAS" | 5

Fig. 1

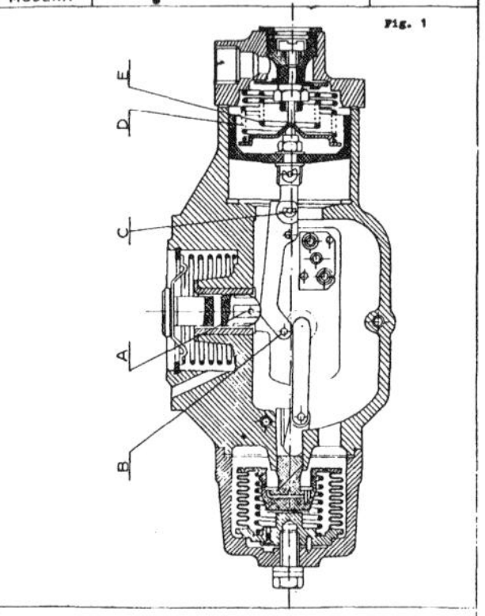

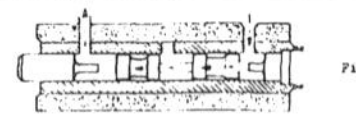

Fig. 2

MASERATI STABILIMENTO COSTRUZIONI INDUSTRIALI MODENA | SAFETY DEVICE FOR INJECTION PUMP | 6

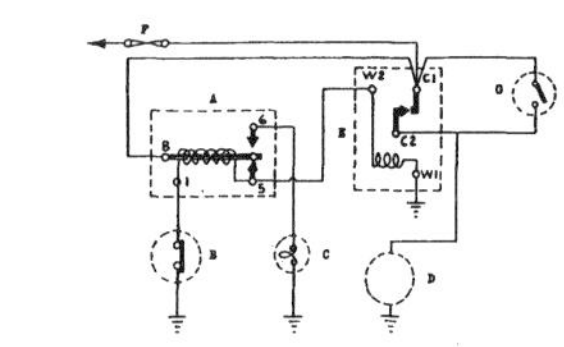

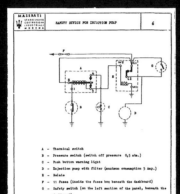

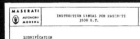

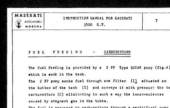

A - Thermical switch
B - Pressure switch (switch off pressure 0,5 atm.)
C - Push button warning light
D - Injection pump with filter (maximum consumption 5 Amp.)
E - Relais
F - 11 fuses (inside the fuses box beneath the dashboard)
G - Safety switch (on the left section of the panel, beneath the dashboard)

MASERATI AUTOMOBILI MODENA | INSTRUCTION MANUAL FOR MASERATI 3500 G.T. | 7

F U E L   F E E D I N G - CARBURETTORS

The fuel feeding is provided by a 2 FP Type LUCAS pump (fig.4) which is sunk in the tank.
The 2 FP pump sucks fuel through one filter (I) situated on the button of the tank (E) and conveys it with pressure the to carburettors (C) eliminating in such a way the inconveniences caused by stagnant gas in the tubes.
The fuel is conveyed to carburettors through a centrifugal pump (D) in line with an electric motor (F) running at 2900 RPM.
The quantity of fuel conveyed varies from 130 to 230 Lt. per hour in accordance with pressure.
Pressure is mantained constant by an exaust valve (B) but can be varied by a screw with nut from 0 to 0,4 Atm.
The pressure is regulated at 0,25 Atm.
The pump is isolated and gets electric current from two wires which gothrough the higher part of the pump and are protected agaist fuel infiltration by a flexible tube fixed to the pump and to the tank.
The fuel filter is situated on the rear right side of the car, and its element (cartridge) is easily replaceable.
Carburattors are Weber 42 DCOE 8 tipe, with double body, mechanical pump and starter.
The three double carburettors suck airthrough a single wide-capacity air filter, with catalytic action.

MASERATI AUTOMOBILI MODENA | POMPA LUCAS 2FP | 8

Fig. 4

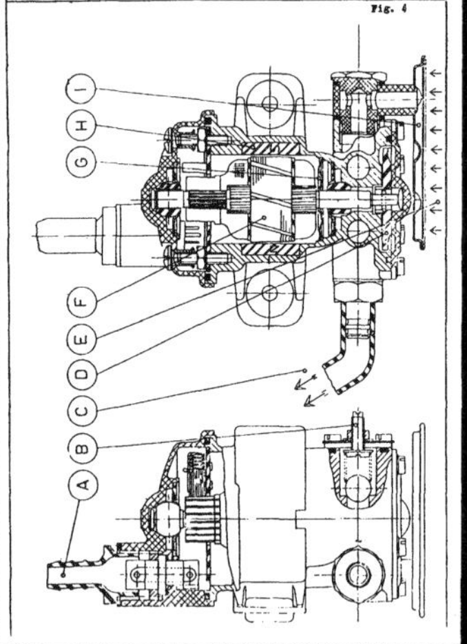

MASERATI AUTOMOBILI MODENA | INSTRUCTION MANUAL FOR MASERATI 3500 G.T. | 9

LUBRIFICATION

Lubrification is by forced circulation through all the main compnents of the engine, and is obtained by mens of a rotor pump situated inside the sump.
the pump sucks oil from the sump, passes it through a filter and then sends it to the components to be lubricated.
to ensure a low oil temperature a small helical pump, immersed in oil, and driven by a V belt circulates the oil through an oilradiator which is situated nex to the water radiator.
The oil filter is located on the right side of the engine block and is desmontable from underneath the car.
The normal oil pressure from low to high revolutions is of 3-5 kilos per sq. cm. (80 - 100 lbs. per sq. inch.).
This pressure is controlled by means of a pressure relief valve installed in the oil filter casting.
Oil is refilled through the pipe union situated on the front of the oil cylinder head.
The level is ascertained by means of a dipstick inserted into the pipe which is situated on the left hand of the sump under the exaust manifold.

COOLING SYSTEM

Engine cooling is obtained by circulating water through an centrifugal pump and a electromagnetic ventilator, the action of which is regulated by a thermometric swich situated on the radiator.
The ventilator comes into action when the water temperature is 75°/86° degrees.
The water flowing through the radiator is also automaticaly regulated by means of a thermostat, fitted on the engine head.
This system permits an Easily heating of the engine, specially at starting.
The water temperature is checked by means of an indicator on the upper section of the radiator.
The water temperature should not exceed 90° degrees.
The graining water tap is placed in the lower section of the radiator.
Radiator capacity is approx. 14 Litres. To the water is added 1% of emulsifiable oil.

MASERATI AUTOMOBILI MODENA | INSTRUCTION MANUAL FOR MASERATI 3500 G.T. | 10

I G N I T I O N   S Y S T E M

The distributor is situated on the front right hand side of the engine, driven by a pair of heliccidal gears and by a battery.
The distributor is a Marelli S - 87 A 12 V 15° (Destro) with automatic advance.
The spark is set at 12° advance. (on crankshaft)
Range of automatic advance is 30° (on crankshaft)
Max. total advance of the coil ignition is 42°.
Firing order is 1 - 5 - 3 - 6 - 2 - 4.
The gap between the breaker points is 0,4 mm. (0,016 in).
Cap between spark plug point is 0,5 mm. (0,02 in)
Diameter and gauge of the plugs are 14 x 11,25 mm.
Marelli type B Z R 201 A coils.

Spark plugs for light duty :	Marelli	CW 240 L
	Bosch	W 215 P 21
	Lodge	2 HL or 3 HLN
	Champion	NA 10
	K L G	FE 80
	Marshal	34 HF
for heavy duty :	Marelli	CW 230 LPS
	Bosch	W 215 P 21
	Champion	NA 12
	Lodge	47 RL
	K L G	FE 250
	Marshal	33 HFS

S T A R T I N G

The starter motor is a Marelli type MT 23 A CV 1,2
Starter is operated by means of a key switch on the dashboard.

E N G I N E   M O U N T S

Engine has an inclination of 4° to the vertical-longitudinal plane, and is offset 38 mm. to the right-hand side.
Engine is mounted on 4 silentblocs.

MASERATI AUTOMOBILI MODENA | INSTRUCTION MANUAL FOR MASERATI 3500 G.T. | 11

T R A N S M I S S I O N

Clutch - The drey spring-loaded single-plate clutch is hydraulically operated by two little pump: one is a 3/4" pump on the pedal and the other is a 7/8" pump on the clutch.
The pedal travel is regulated by means of a screw nut situated on the strut of the inlet side of the pump.

GEAR-BOX - There are 4 or 5 forward speed and a reverse ones.
There is syncromesh in all forward gears.
The gear lever is situated directly on the top centre of the gear box.

Gear ratios :	Normal
1 ratio	0,331 = 3,02
2 "	0,540 = 1,85
3 "	0,776 = 1,29
4 "	1 = 1
5 "	1,18 = 0,85
Reverse	0,315 = 3,17

A X L E

Rear axle is a rigid hypoid - bevels.

The normal reduction ratio is :	13 / 49 = 3,77
It can be substitued by :	13 / 43 = 3,31
	13 / 46 = 3,54
	11 / 45 = 4,09

C H A S S I S

Principal dimension :

Front tread		1390	mm	(54,3 in.)
Rear tread		1360	mm	(53,5 in.)
Wheel base	Coupé	2600	mm	(102,3 in.)
	Coupé S. . . .	2500	mm	(98,4 in.)
	Convertible . . .	2500	mm	(98,4 in.)
Ground clearence		130	mm	(5,1 in.)
Weight of the empty car		1300	kilos	(2750 lbs.)
Weight laden		1400	kilos	(3100 lbs.)

The frame is exceptionally rigid and is made of longitudunal and transverse members, which are tubolar and eliptical in shape.
The size and strength of those members is proportional to the stress which they will undergo.

MASERATI AUTOMOBILI MODENA | INSTRUCTION MANUAL FOR MASERATI 3500 G.T. | 12

F R O N T   S U S P E N S I O N

Front suspension is a quadrilateral transverse type with coil springs and with pivots acting on rubber suspensions.
Telescopic shock absorber type Girling F 4.5 or Koni 82.1019.
There is a transverse stabilizer bar to limit roll angle.

R E A R   S U S P E N S I O N

Rear suspension is by Cantilever leaf springs, with 2 Girling F 7,5 shock absorbers.
There is a transverse stabilizer bar which steadies the car when cornering.

S T E E R I N G

The steering box is mounted on the left hand side and is of the type with variable play.
It is operated through a column with a flexible joint to dampen vibrations, and acts directly on the steering bars through a double lever.
The toe-in of the front wheels is between 5 and 6 mm.
The min. turning radius is 6 meters (20 feet).

B R A K E S

The brakes are hydraulic acting on all four wheels with 305 mm. diameter disc brakes at the front and 291 mm. diameter disc brakes at the rear.
The braking surface in the front wheels is 294,5 squared inches and 186 squared inches in the rear.
The adjustment of the brake pads is automatical.
A second mechanical braking system, operates on the rear disc brakes.
This braking system is used as an additional safety braking, when parking, by pulling a hand-lever.
The braking system is equipped with a vacuum control situated on the right hand side of the engine which reduces the foot pressure required on the brake pedal to a minimum.
A vacuum of approx; 280 mm of mercury is obtained in the servo brake chamber by connecting this unit to the inlet manifold of the engine.

W H E E L S

The wheels discs are 550 X 16, perforated and attached to the hub by means of 4 [illegible] bolts.

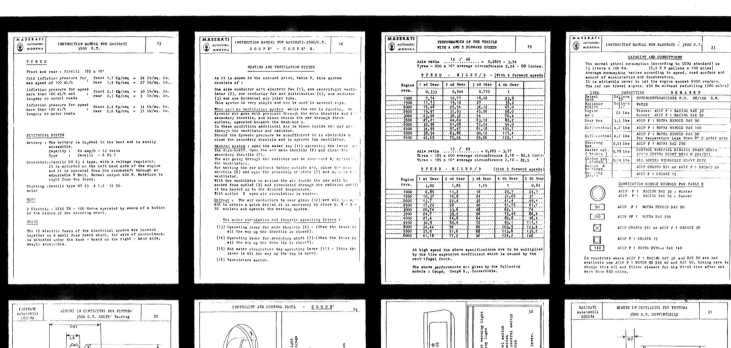
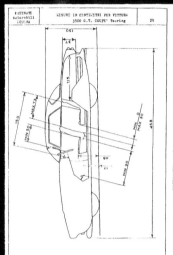
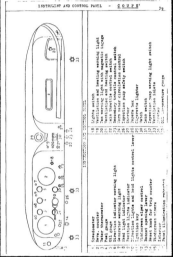
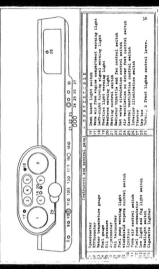
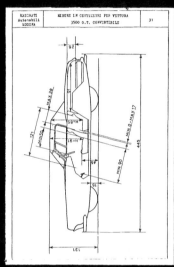

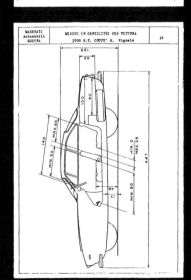
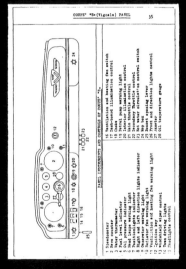
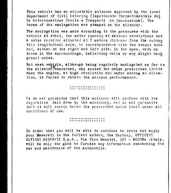

Instruction manual for the GT, GTI and first series GTIS (Sebring). The sheets were simple photocopies!

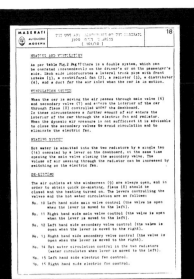
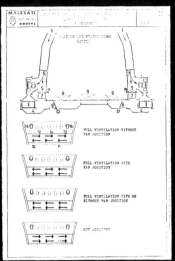
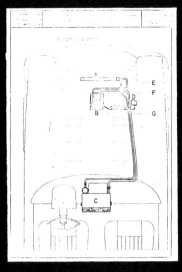
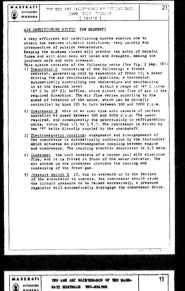

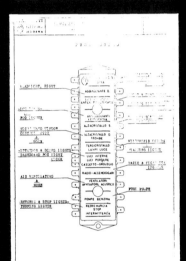

A 28-page manual on the Sebring with either 3·5 or 3·7-litre engine. Four pages were devoted to the heating system!

Handbook for the Mistral in all engine capacities. The chapter on automatic transmissions concerned Mistral while the lubrication schedules referred to Mistrale

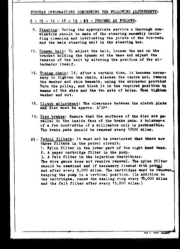
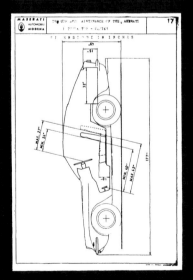
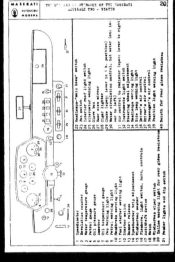

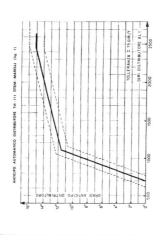

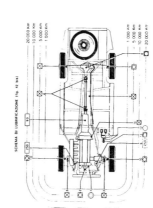

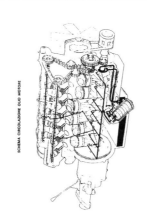

The first model with a proper
and conventional driver's
handbook was the Mistral

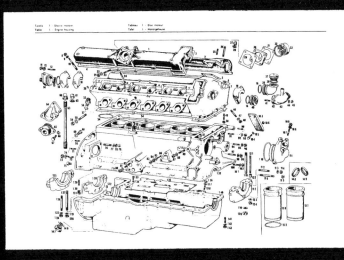

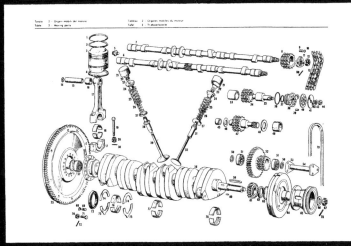

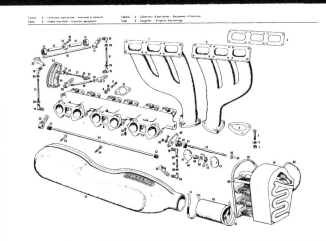

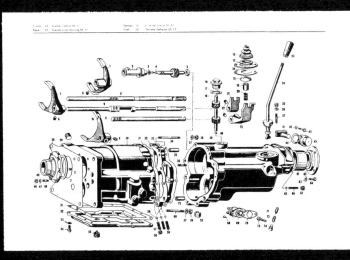

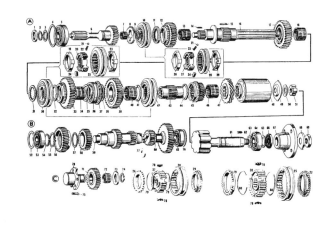

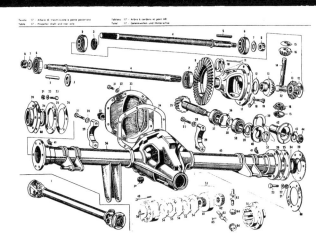

Issued to distributors only, the spare
parts book on the 3500 series covered
every permutation including the first
series Sebring

A very early brochure's exquisite art work advertises the A6 1500. Its cover is below left

3500GTI series II by Touring of Milan

3500GTI series I by Sebring by Vignale   3500GTI spider by Vignale

4-litre Mistral coupé by Frua

4.7-litre Quattraporte by Frua

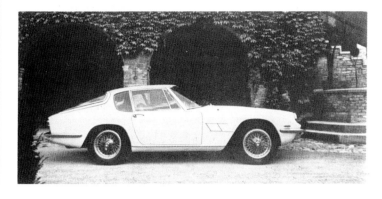

MASERATI DUE POSTI

A typical spread from the Mistral brochure

Maserati's fold-out for the Indy, Ghibli
(coupé and spider) and Mexico

4.7-litre Mexico by Vignale

All in colour and beautifully done:
Indy for America

4.9-litre Ghibli coupé and spider by Ghia

4.7-litre Indy America by Vignale

Bora by Ital Design

1972 production — Mexico, Ghibli, Indy, Bora

Merak by Ital Design

Merak SS by Ital Design

Prototypes of the Khamsin by Bertone

Boomerang by Ital Design

Maserati coupé by Ital Design

A strangely poetical colour brochure for the Khamsin

Maserati Quattroporte II

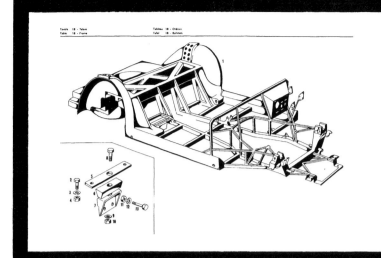

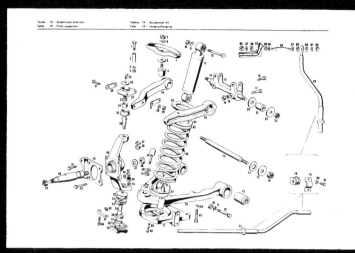

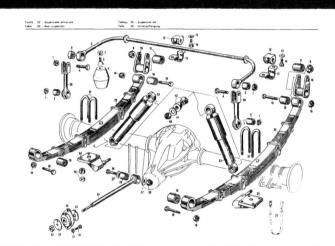

MASERATI 2 POSTI

PARTI DI RICAMBIO   *PIECES DE RECHANGE*

SPARE PARTS   *ERSATZTEILE*

OFFICINE ALFIERI MASERATI S.P.A.
MODENA (ITALIA)
VIA CIRO MENOTTI, 322 - TEL. 30-101 (3 LINEE)

The 2-posti (Mistral) parts manual did a
similar job and included the 4-litre

MASERATI 3500 G.T.
A CARBURATORI E INIEZIONE

PARTI DI RICAMBIO

SPARE PARTS   *ERSATZTEILE*

PIECES DE RECHANGE   *PIEZAS DE REPUESTO*

OFFICINE ALFIERI MASERATI S.P.A.
MODENA (ITALIA)
VIA CIRO MENOTTI, 322 - TELEF. 30-101

PART·3
The V8s and V6s—1959 to 1979

The 5-litre

First exhibited in 1959 with coachwork from Touring of Milan, the 5000GT was in effect a civilised version of the formidable Tipo 450S sports racing car. This powerful V8 Maserati engine first came to light in 1956 from the basic design by Ing. Bellentani in 1954/55. While the factory used it as a 4200 and 4500 cc engine in their competition cars, it was also offered as a 5·7 and 6·4-litre, the latter for marine use by Guidotti in his water speed attempts. Presumably when the factory ceased racing in 1958 there were some V8 *motores* lying around at Modena collecting the dust. These were given new life when Ing. Alfieri refined the unit for normal road use, although it was never to be intended for series production. Many people showed interest in this rugged four-overhead camshaft engine, so when the factory let some select coachbuilders exercise their individual talents around the V8, the customers were very special; among them Briggs Cunningham, the Shah of Persia, Sig. Agnelli, Sig. Innocenti and the Aga Khan.

The first three models would seem to have had the gear-drive camshaft engines developing 345 bhp at 5700 rpm, with a combination of front disc and rear drum brakes. Certainly these cars were on Weber carburettors and with four speed transmission. I strongly suspect the chassis was nothing more than a strengthened 3500 frame with all the usual bought-out parts hung on it. International journalist Bernard Cahier carried out a road test in 1961 and reported the story in *Sports Car Graphic* the following year. The model he exercised was the Ghia version, which was number 018, the ninth one constructed. Cahier reported that the car had all the comforts and refinements of the most luxurious of automobiles, but called it a sports touring car. While driving on the Autostrada de Sol he recorded a speed of 152 mph and was informed by a casual Bertocchi that many more 'revs' were available. In fact, Maserati's chief test driver had completed several test runs with Hans Tanner on a previous occasion and managed a top speed of over 170 mph. Both journalists confirmed the chassis was rock steady at these high speeds, but strangely they were disillusioned about the sensation of speed. Cahier even suggested it was nothing different to travelling at 90 mph; some selling feature!

More than a match for the Ferrari Superfast, customers were a small group of rich connoisseurs who were looking for precisely this type of automobile. Orsi let the car be marketed from 1959 to late 1964 completing a mere 32 examples, but probably consuming all those surplus V8 power units!

Stylised front end of the Shah of Persia's 5000GT by Touring of Milan

The Shah's Maserati pictured in Switzerland during 1972 some years after he had sold it. This car is now living in Indiana and is chassis number 002

139

The second 5-litre has also found a sunnier climate in South Africa. The first owner Basil Read purchased it from the factory in 1960 although it is a 1959 model

The third attempt by Touring of Milan on chassis number 006
was sold to Germany in late 1962 although built in 1961

The Turin show car of 1959
was the second 5000GT
Maserati built by Touring of
Milan. Chassis number 004

Designed by Pininfarina on the 5-litre
for Gianni Agnelli in 1961 but built by
Scaglietti. This is 008, the fourth model
of the series

A thoughtful Bertocchi after a run up the autostrada in an Allemano bodied 5000GT—1961

Reputedly shown by Vignale at the 1961 Turin Show, if correct, was the only convertible on the 5000GT chassis. Factory records for the type 103 do not credit Vignale with having built such a car

5000GT production

AM103.002	Touring of Milan	Shah of Persia	October 1959
AM103.004	Touring of Milan	Basil Read	March 1960
AM103.006	Touring of Milan	Rolf Helm	September 1962
AM103.008	Pinin Farina	Sig. Agnelli	April 1961
AM103.010	Touring of Milan	Fonderia di Modenai	June 1961
AM103.012	Monterosa	Filippo Montanari	November 1961
AM103.014	Allemano	William Brown	October 1961
AM103.016	Michelotti	Briggs Cunningham	June 1962
AM103.018	Ghia	Sig. Innocenti	August 1961
AM103.020	Allemano	Agency Maserati-Paris	October 1961
AM103.022	Allemano	Alfonso Lopez	December 1961
AM103.024	Allemano	Dea SpA	March 1962
AM103.026	Allemano	Belponer	January 1964
AM103.028	Allemano	Immobilaire Monte Carlo	March 1962
AM103.030	Allemano	Pavonlelli & Gaetavo	February 1962
AM103.032	Allemano	Pier Franceto Martini	August 1963
AM103.034	Allemano	Marcel Leclef	April 1962
AM103.036	Allemano	Merz & Popst	March 1963
AM103.038	Allemano	Martinelli & Sonvico	May 1963
AM103.040	Allemano	Martinelli & Sonvico	April 1962
AM103.042	Allemano	Auto O'Farril	April 1962
AM103.044	Allemano	Bonetti	June 1962
AM103.046	Allemano	Merli Brandini Maria Piero	December 1963
AM103.048	Frua	Instituto Farmoco Terapico	November 1963
AM103.050	Allemano	Martinelli & Sonvico	July 1963
AM103.052	Allemano	Martinelli & Sonvico	April 1963
AM103.054	Allemano	Guiseppe Comola	September 1962
AM103.056	Allemano	Martinelli & Sonvico	May 1963
AM103.058	Allemano	Auto-Paris	April 1964
AM103.060	Frua	Aga Khan	August 1962
AM103.062	Bertone	Gian Carlo Guasti	January 1964
AM103.066		Auto-König, Germany	October 1964

TOTAL 32 cars

Records do not show 064 as having been built and no coachbuilder for chassis 066 which could have been the mysterious spider by Vignale, or another Allemano

One of the best looking 5000GT Maseratis came from Bertone in 1962

142

From Carrozzeria Frua in 1962 for the Aga Khan on chassis
number 060

From Allemano on a fuel injection 5-litre in 1961/62. He
titled this version Indianapolis

144

The normal Allemano version on a 5000GT. He incorporated
rectangular lamps on all his Maserati creations after this

Chassis number 056, a 1963 model. Note twin quarter lights
and wheel spinners which were for a spanner not hammer!

A handsome 5-litre by Monterosa reputedly on chassis 012
for an Italian gentleman

Three-spoke Nardi wheel through which one could glimpse
the time or see how fast the Maserati was moving. This is 056

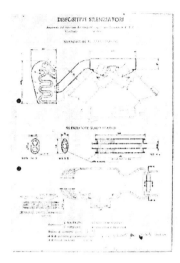
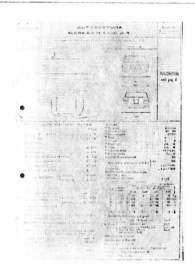
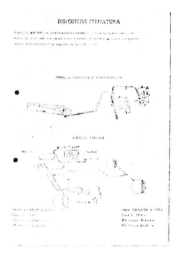

A copy of the Ministry of Transport certificate for the Tipo 103 or 5000GT dated 1961

149

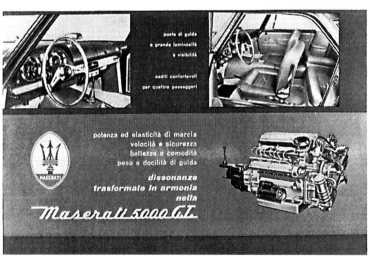

Probably a very accurate artist's impression of a 5-litre
Maserati in motion. This brochure depicts an Allemano
version with fuel injection engine and four-speed gearbox

MAIN CHARACTERISTICS AND DATA

ENGINE

Number of cylinders	8 90° V
Bore and stroke	98,5 x 81 mm.
Individual cylinder capacity	616,91 cc.
Total Capacity	4935,33
Max. power	350 HP.
Taxable power	47,2 HP.
Compression ratio . . . . ;	8,2 : 1

Cylinder block is of light alloy with liners of special cast iron.
Cylinder heads are made of a light alloy with overhead valves, in
which the valve seats have been inserted.
Combustion chambers are hemispherical.
The crankshaft is dynamically balanced and is supported by five lead-
indium alloy bearings.
The conrods are made of forged steel in H section with the big-end
bearing made of lead-indium alloy. The little end bearing is a bronze
bush.
Pistons are made of light alloy with two compression rings and two
oil rings.

DISTRIBUTION

The inclined valves in the head are actuated by 4 overhead camshafts
driven by helical gears. Valves are operated directly by the camshaft
with the interposition of rocker arms. Valve clearance is by means of
screws and back nuts. The proper clearance (cold) between rolling rocker arm and the base radius of the lobe of cam are :

lift of the inlet valve at top dead centre = 0,2 mm - A.A. 61° - RA 90°
lift of the exaust valve at top dead centre = 0,250 mm - A.S. 90° - RSJO°

INLET MANIFOLD

Petrol is pumped from the tank by means of two FISPA electric pumps.
The tank is fitted with a float indicating the petrol level.
The petrol filter is situated on the right hand side and immediately
in back of the electric pump and is fitted with an easily replaceable
cartridge.
Carburation is by means of three twin Weber type 45 IDM with mechanical
pump.
Carburettors take air trough one larger filter.

LUBRICATION

Lubrication is by forced circulation through all the main components of
the engine, and is obtained by means of a rotor pump situated inside
the sump. The pump sucks oil from the sump, passes it through a filter
and then sends it to the components to be lubricated.
To ensure a low oil temperatire a small helical pump, immersed in oil,
and driven by a V belt circulates the oil through an oil radiator which
is situated next to the water radiator.

The filter, with two filtering cartridges, is easily accessible.
The normal oil pressure from low to high revolutions is of 3 - 5
kilos per sq. cm. (80 - 100 lbs. per sq. inch). This pressure is
controlled by means of a pressure releif valve installed in the oil
filter itself.
Oil is realaced though the pipe union situated on the front of the
oil cylinder head.
The level is ascertained by means of a dipstick inscrted in the pipe
which is situated on the right hand side of the sump.

Oil capacity is approx. 13 liters - (3 gallons)

COOLING SYSTEM

Engine cooling is obtained by circulating water with two centrifugal
pumps and a fan driven directly by distribution gears.
Water flows through the radiator and is regulated by means of two ther-
mostats situated on the pipes to radiator.
This thermostat facilitates the warming up of the endine especialy when
starting. The temperature of the water is measured by means of an indicator on the dash board connected to a thermoelctric bulb, which is inserted into the upper part of the radiator.
The temperature of the water should not exceed 90° c. (190° F).
The draining water tap is placed in the lower portion of the radiator.
Radiator capacity is approx. 15 liters.

IGNITION SYSTEM

The actuation of ignition is actuated by two distributors situated on
the front side of the engine, driven by helical gears and fed by a batte-
ry.
Distributors are MARELLI 7073 DTEM with automatic advance.
The spark is set at 12° advance.
Range of automatic advance is 30°.
Max. total advance of the coil ignition is 42°.
Firing order is : 1 - 5 - 4 - 2 - 6 - 3 - 7 - 8.
The gap between the breaker points is 0.4 mm. (0.016 in.)
Gap between spark plug points is 0.5 mm. (0.02 in.)
Diameter and gauge of the plugs are 14 x 1.25 mm.
MARELLI type SB 11 DT. coils

Sparke plugs for light duty : Marelli 250 B
                              Bosch 250 TB
                              Lodge 2 HL or 3 HLN
                              Campion NA 10
                              KLG FE 80
                              Marshal 34 HF

for heavy duty :
                              Marelli CBW 1000 B
                              Bosch 270 T2
                              Champion NA 12
                              Lodge 47 RL
                              KLG FE 250
                              Marshal 33 HFS

INJECTION

Twin carburetors	45 IDM
Max jet	165
stop screw	200
pumps	50
Minimus	65
air choke	37
Nozzle	3,5
Sump F. 2	7,8
Air intake horns	49 x 58

STARTING

The starter motor is a MARELLI type 41 B CV 2,5.
The starter is operated by means of a key switch on the dashboard.

ENGINE MOUNTS

Engine is situated longitudinaly to the plane of the car, and it is mounted
on 4 silentblocs.

TRANSMISSION

Clutch - The dray spring-loaded double plate clutch is hydraulically ope-
rated by two little pumps: one is a 3/4" pump on the pedal and the other
is a 7/8" pump on the clutch.
The pedal travel is reglated by means of a screw nut situated on the
strut of the inlet side of the pump.
There are 4 forward speeds and a reverse one.
There is a syncromesh in all forward gears.
The gear lever is situated directly on the top centre of the gear box.

Gear ratio:

1 ratio	2,279
2 "	1,685
3 "	1,273
4 "	1
RG "	3,875

AXLE

Rear axle is a rigid hypoid-type with two conical shafts.
The normal reduction ratio is: 13/46 = 3,54 - 0,282
It can be replaced with : ......13/43 = 3,31 - 0,302
                          "   13/49 = 3,77 - 0,265
                          "   12/49 = 4,09 - 0,244
                          "   11/47 = 4,27 - 0,234
                          "   11/50 = 4,55 - 0,219
                          "   11/53 = 4,78 - 0,190

CHASSIS

Main dimensions :
Front tread   1390 mm.
Rear "   1360 mm (53,5 inc.)
Wheel base   260 mm (102 inc.)

Minimum heigh from ground	110 mm.
Weight of the empty car	1500 Kilos
Weight of leaden car	1600 Kilos

The frame is exeptionaly rigid and is made of longitudiral and transverse
members, which are tubular and eliptical in shape.
The size and strength of these members is proportional to the stress
which they will undergo.

FRONT SUSPENSION

Front suspension is a quadrilateral transverse type with coil springs
and with pivots acting on rubber suspensions.
Telescopic shock absorber type GIRLING F. 4.5 or KONI B2. 1019.
There is a transverse stabilizer bar to counteract sway.

REAR SUSPENSION

Rear suspension is by cantiliver springs, with 2 Girling F. 7,5 shock
absorbers.
There is a transverse stabilizer bar which steadies the car when cornering.

STEERING

The steering box is mounted on the left hand side and is of the type
with variable play.
It is operated through a column with a flexible joint to dampen vibrations, and act directly on the steering bars trough a double lever.
The toe-in of the front wheels is between 5 and 6 mm. The minimum
turning radius is 5,3 meters.

BRAKES

The brakes are hydraulic acting on all four wheels with disc brakes at
the front and drum brakes at the rear. Rear drum brakes measure 305 x
76 mm. (12" x 3").
The front brakes have an automatic adjustement while the rear brakes
are adjusted by cams situated on the brake plate.
Clearance must be 0.3 mm. (0.012").
Rear brakes are also mechanicaly operated by means of a hand lever located under the dashboard.
The braking system is equipped with a vacuum control situated on the
right hand side of the engine which reduces the foot pressure required on
the brake pedal minimum.
A vacuum of approx. 280 mm. of mercury is obtained in the servo brake
chamber by connecting this unit to the inlet manifold of the engine.

WHEELS

The wheel discs are 550 x 16, perforated and attached to the hub by means
of 4 stud bolts.

TYRES

Front and rear: Pirelli 6.50 x 16 - Continental or Firestone 6.00 x 16

Pressure cold { front 1.6 kilos sq. cm.
              { Rear 1,6 sq. cm.

Pressure for sport use: front and rear 2,2 Kilos sq. cm.

HORN

Two MARELLI silver-type TT 11 C horns, operated by means of a button
in the centre of the steering wheel.

FUSES

The 12 electric fuses of the electrical system are located together
on a small fuse board which, for sake and convenience, i situated under
the dash-board on the right-hand side , easily accessible.

VEHICLE'S PERFORMANCES

Axle ratio .... 13/46 - 0,2825 - 3,54
Tyres: 6,50 x 16" - Average circumference 2,3 meters - at 200 Kms/h

SPEED : Kms/h

Engine revs.	1st gear 2,279 0,479	2nd gear 1,685 0,594	3rd gear 1,273 0,786	4th gear 1
1000	17,05	23,1	30,6	38,9
1500	25,6	34,6	45,9	58,3
2000	34,1	46,1	61,2	77,8
2500	42,6	57,7	76,5	97,2
3000	51,5	69,2	91,8	116,7
3500	59,7	80,7	10,7	136,6
4000	68,2	92,2	122,5	155,6
4500	76,7	103,7	137,7	175
5000	85,2	115,3	153	194
5500	93,8	126,7	168	220
6000	102,3	138,4	183	241
6500	110,8	149,9	199	258

BORE OVERSIZES

BORE	STROKE	PISTON AREA	INDIVIDUAL C.C.	TOTAL C.C.
98,5	81	sq.mm. 7620,149	cubic cm. 617,231	cubic cm. 4937,848
98,75	81	sq.mm. 7658,875	cubic cm. 620,368	cubic cm. 4962,944
99	81	sq.mm. 7697,705	cubic cm. 623,514	cubic cm. 4988,112
99,25	81	sq.mm. 7736,629	cubic cm. 626,667	cubic cm. 5013,336
99,5	81	sq.mm. 7775,654	cubic cm. 629,828	cubic cm. 5038,624
99,75	81	sq.mm. 7814,777	cubic cm. 632,996	cubic cm. 5063,975
100	81	sq.mm. 7854,000	cubic cm. 636,174	cubic cm. 5089,392

COMBUSTION CHAMBER VOLUME

Compression ratio.

7,5	= 94,958 (cubic cm.)
7,75	= 91,441
8	= 88,175
8,25	= 85,135
8,5	= 82,294
8,75	= 79,642
9	= 77,157
9,25	= 74,815
9,50	= 72,615
9,75	= 70,540
10,0	= 61,723

In the 5000GT handbook Maserati left
you in no doubt as to what you had got.
'This is because the engine at high
revolutions while accelerating swiftly
can exceed the legal limit. This is
unavoidable if the car is to perform with
the speed characteristics of this vehicle'.

The front-engined eights

Maserati offered at the 1963 Turin Show a four door, four seater saloon or berlina. This example, the only one built in that year, had a 4-litre V8 engine which was soon replaced with the 4136 cc (88 × 85 mm) unit.

The Quattroporte (or four door) had a five-speed ZF transmission with optional three-speed automatic from Borg-Warner. In addition the usual extras such as air conditioning and power steering were available. One problem with this model was its rear suspension design which incorporated a De Dion set up. Why Orsi gave this design to a production car is not known, as the tooling costs must have been uneconomic, but that was the least of his problems. The idea of a high speed saloon was in itself what the motoring public wanted but probably not in the style of the Quattroporte. The coachwork by Frua, in steel, was not inspiring and the interior layout and fittings were not so special for a car costing 13,000 US dollars. However the V8 motor would push this heavyweight, almost 4000 lb, to 130 mph only at the expense of petrol consumption.

From November 1965 Maserati offered an uprated version which had the 4719 cc engine developing 290 bhp at maximum 5500 rpm. That suspect rear suspension was changed in favour of a normal live rear axle arrangement, and Frua obliged with some major interior refinements. Externally the second series had twin circular headlamps similar to the Sebring. The factory were a little undecided about its designation sometimes titling this one 107/A, 107/2 or 107/47. *Sports Car Graphic* drove a 4200 Quattroporte in September 1968, which strangely still had a De Dion rear end in a series II body shape. The factory playing the fox again! The road tester had little to say about this saloon except that in his opinion a 14,000 US dollar car should at least look like one, he gave it zero marks for styling and comfort.

The Quattroporte was phased out in 1969 and certainly it never was one of Orsi's better models, with sales being universally disappointing.

Continuing the V8 theme and running concurrently with the Quattroporte, was the two door coupé Mexico introduced in 1966. Coachwork was from Vignale and this model had special appeal for four people travelling comfortably at high speed in a Maserati that had considerable style and elegance. Certainly, it had more to offer than the Quattroporte. As usual the initial versions had the 4200 cc V8 followed by the 4·7 litre developing 290 bhp. The total weight was around 3400 lb and the car was definitely capable of high speed cruising with little criticism of the handling and ride. Customers were mostly from France and Switzerland although the home market did take some cars. Why so few Mexicos were constructed is not known but this model was also phased out with the Quattroporte in

1968. For a Maserati that appeared to be popular at the time, it is now difficult to comprehend Orsi's marketing policy with regard to these two not dissimilar models. That is assuming such a policy existed at all!

Sketches from the desk of Giugiaro in late 1965 resulted in Carrozzeria Ghia displaying a Maserati Ghibli coupé at the 1966 Turin Show. Looking like the wind it was named after, this new model was for the factory 'doing what came naturally'. The coupé caused a sensation in 1966 and had an appreciative audience until its demise in early 1973. Certainly the highest consumer of Ghiblis was America where it is still held in high regard by motoring enthusiasts. Offered with the now standard V8 Maserati engine with improved water porting in the cylinder heads, in either 4·7 or 4·9 litre form and installed in the usual chassis, the car was strictly a two seater. A five speed gearbox or automatic transmission was optional while standard were the wishbone and coil spring front suspension with normal rear axle on semi-elliptic springs with anti-roll bars front and rear. The completed car weighed in excess of 3900 lb, not unobviously assisted by the steel coachwork, but it could achieve the standing quarter mile in 17·7 seconds with an ultimate velocity of 160 mph.

Apart from no rear legroom the other minus quality was no neck room for the roofline was extremely low, overall height being a mere 46 inches. The four headlamps were raised electrically, although some said too slowly for safety. The Ghibli could certainly stop when required being fitted with twin-servo assisted ventilated discs with three pistons per caliper.

On the road the Ghibli seemed to enjoy many compliments for its looks and performance. If there were any shortcomings it was a tendency for the front end to lift slightly at high speed; spoilers were not the vogue. An American magazine in 1968 said of this model, 'The Ghibli is by far Maserati's greatest contribution to the automotive world in the past 20 years. Its appearance alone gives one a feeling of opulence.'

While customers were hurrying for the coupé in 1967 and 1968, Ghia brought forth his spider version in 1969. The car was immediately heralded as a classic design, its flowing line somehow enhanced with a soft top. The folding hood was concealed under a panel in the rear and could be easily erected or stowed in a couple of minutes. Elegance had arrived for Maserati with this lovely spider, unfortunately a mere 125 examples were completed during its production span.

An increasing demand for a Maserati with the looks akin to a Ghibli but with seating for four with luggage, brought forth the Indy from Vignale in 1968. Production commenced in 1969, orders being encouraged by showing the model at Geneva in that year. Initially

151

only available as a 4200, these examples were without power steering as standard equipment which was a tiring mistake. The rear suspension was as usual unsophisticated with semi-elliptic springs and Salisbury rear axle, additionally located by a short torque rod mounted in rubber bushes. Interior noise level was low and the body style proved to have excellent aerodynamics, which was maybe why it had the smaller capacity V8.

The Indy could comfortably transport four people at 150 mph with a fuel consumption of 15 mpg. Orsi decided to offer this model with the 4200 V8 until 1972 when the 4700 was introduced in the chassis. Customers for this good looking fast-back were world wide even with a price of more than 9000 pounds Sterling. It was almost the factory's top volume production model coming second only to the Ghibli, which emphasises that output during the period 1969/1974 reached over 2000 front engine V8s completed.

Front-engined V8 production

Quattroporte 4200/4700	Frua	1963	1 car
		1964	83 cars
		1965	149 cars
		1966	113 cars
		1967	193 cars
		1968	140 cars
		1969	80 cars
		TOTAL	759 cars
Mexico 4200/4700	Vignale	1966	15 cars
		1967	97 cars
		1968	138 cars
		TOTAL	250 cars
Ghibli 4700/4900	Ghia coupé	1967	87 cars
		1968	276 cars
		1969	270 cars
		1970	216 cars
		1971	158 cars
		1972	137 cars
		1973	5 cars
	Ghia spider	1969	21 cars
		1970	62 cars
		1971	27 cars
		1972	15 cars
		TOTAL	1274 cars
Indy 4200/4700/4900	Vignale	1969	83 cars
		1970	263 cars
		1971	276 cars
		1972	246 cars
		1973	221 cars
		1974	47 cars
		TOTAL	1136 cars

The prototype Quattroporte on the factory scrapheap in
1971. This was chassis number 1092

An early 4-door back from a test drive
and some trials round the Modena track

The 4-door berlina from Frua was a follow-on from the 5000GT although considerably more docile

Rectangular headlamps were later replaced with individual circular ones on the series II

A Mexico coming off the production line in 1966. Note normal Borrani wire wheels

154

The V8 engine on Weber carburettors in the Quattroporte. Although each cylinder head could accommodate eight spark plugs, it was always finished with a single plug per cylinder and a Bosch distributor. The substantial air filter box was made of glass fibre

Mexico interior design was similar to the series II Quattroporte; air conditioning was optional

The Mexico, from Vignale, was in effect a two-door version of the Quattroporte having the same seating capacity. This is chassis number 042, a 4.7 litre version

Clean rear end with rubber inserts in over-riders. The boot was opened by lever inside the car

Exhibited at the 1971 Geneva Show, the wire wheels were bolt-on type with safety conscious spinners

On test, December 1966, a 4·7 litre Ghibli. Note rear light
treatment which was not adopted for series production

V8 installation in a 4700 Ghibli. The plastic piping from the
air cleaner has not yet been fitted

The 'old man' relaxing at the wheel of a 1966 Ghibli.
Bertocchi adopted the cap and suede jacket in the late 1960s
in place of his overalls, while road testing

A 1971 Ghibli SS using some rubber on its way to the
autostrada. The SS meant a lighter, more powerful car with a
dry sump engine. Little more can be confirmed

In European trim, the Ghibli was certainly a handsome coupé.
It could go as well, although its high speed handling was in
some doubt

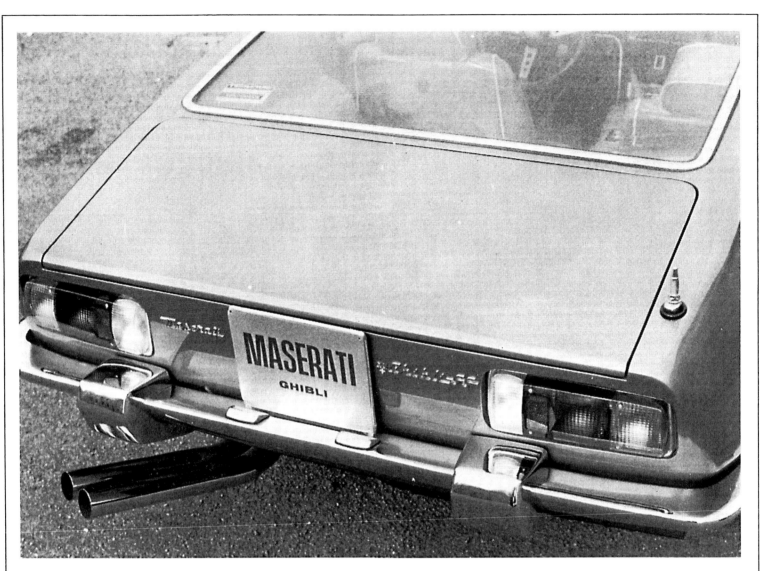

1971 Ghibli SS ready for display at some motor show. The
small rear window sticker confirms it is fitted with air
conditioning

Pictured outside the factory in 1971; note the additional side
turn indicators and new style wheels from Campagnola

The 1969 Ghibli spider was a gorgeous looking Maserati;
Carrozzeria Ghia got full marks for this creation

Sitting in the sun where it undoubtedly was at home!

162

Resting on the Maserati stand at the 1970 Turin Show is a
4900 Ghibli SS spider. The bolt-on wire wheels did much for
the looks but were an expensive option

Interior of the Turin Show car. Can you really believe that
someone asked for automatic transmission?

163

164

Cutaway drawing of the 1969 Maserati Indy. The point of the smaller drawing is to show the fully adjustable steering column

Different tail light treatment and the required side turn indicators beneath the front and rear bumpers mark this Indy for the US market

All the flaps open. A 1971 model fitted with air conditioning and power steering which was essential for this heavyweight

Not the Maserati service manager, nor Bertocchi's sister, but a publicity extra for a 1970 Indy

Plenty of room in the rear although accessibility was not for the clumsy

Vignale had something to show off with the Indy, a genuine
four-seater GT. The air vents near the windscreen later
disappeared

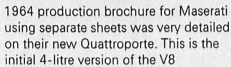

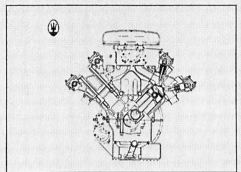

1964 production brochure for Maserati
using separate sheets was very detailed
on their new Quattroporte. This is the
initial 4-litre version of the V8

The 4-porte brochure for the first series models
with a De Dion rear axle

MASERATI 🚗 MEXICO

MASERATI 🚗 GHIBLI

Again the 'landscape' brochure, this time for the series II Quattroporte now with refined interior fittings and wood veneer dash panel

This 1970 brochure is unexciting without colour and shows a 4·2-litre version of this practical four seater GT

At the time of its announcement many considered the Mexico to be a tarted-up QP. It was, however, a high quality prestige model for the factory with wire wheels as standard fitting

A rare and desirable automobile, the Ghibli spider had almost everything in its favour. This catalogue was dated late 1969 for the following year's sales

A brochure for the 'shorter' Ghibli, it was unlikely the lady came with the car!

The factory brochure for the 1970 Ghibli which somehow increased in overall length by 100 mm. The instrument layout is changed although still resembling an aircraft panel. Who purchased such a model with automatic transmission?

MASERATI 🚗 INDY

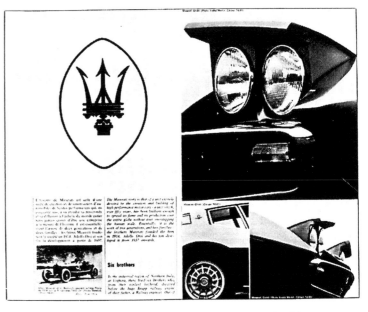

'édition spéciale' of Société Citroën's *Le Double Chevron* house magazine was published to commemorate their takeover of the Maserati company. It was beautifully produced to tell the story of Maserati both in French and English. Its final words were 'Maserati-Citroën is an alliance between two firms which stand out in the motor-car field.'

One engine configuration, in either 4·2 or 4·7 litres, propelling three different models. The factory photographers always used elegant settings for their cars

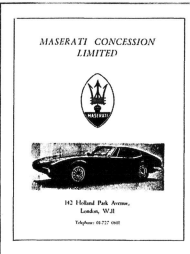

The UK concessionaire produced his own sales brochure.
On the reverse he admitted them to be expensive though
desirable cars

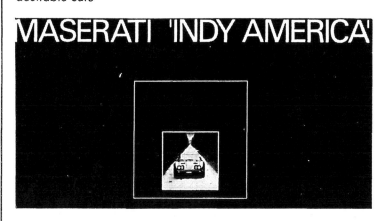

I can only assume the Indy America had a special meaning
for the United States market. It was not a feature that the
essential power steering continued as an optional extra

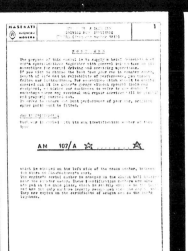

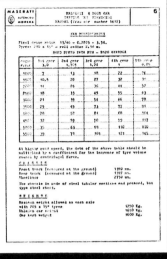

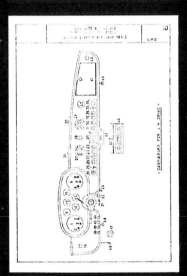
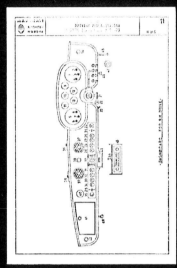

The Quattroporte handbook from chassis number 1412 which appeared to be the first 4·7 version

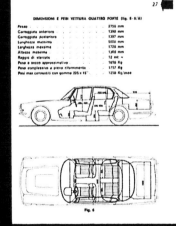
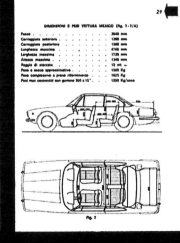
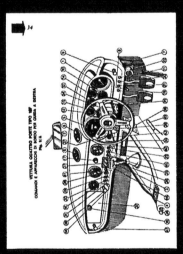

An 'economy' maintenance handbook for two models. The factory did not manage to print a coloured wiring diagram, which was confusing

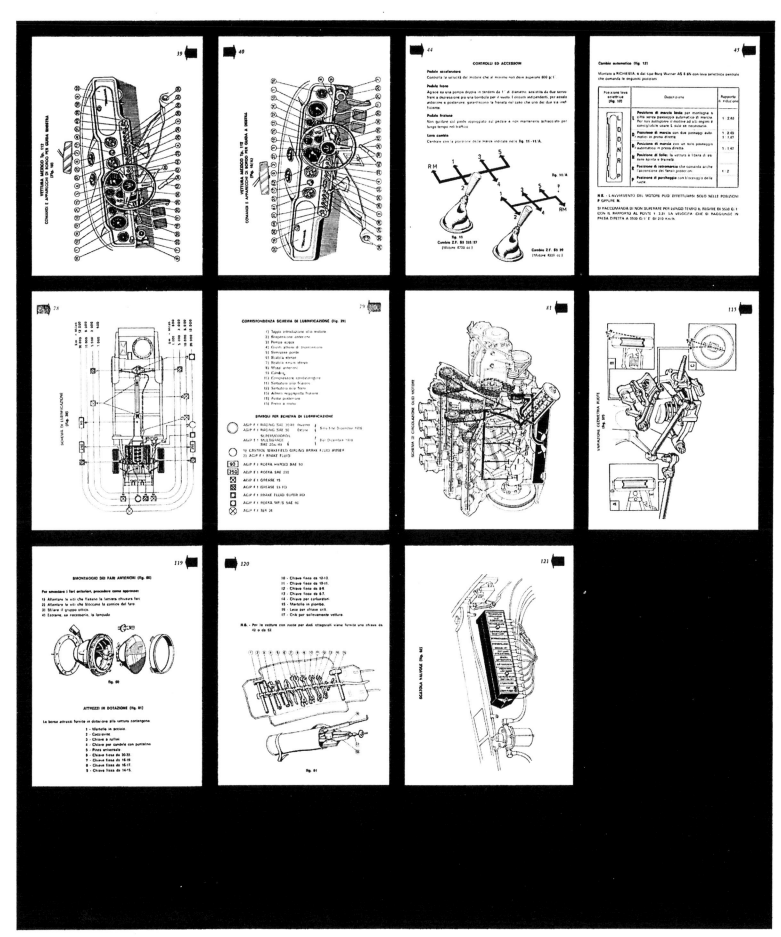

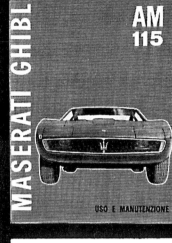

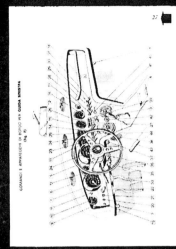
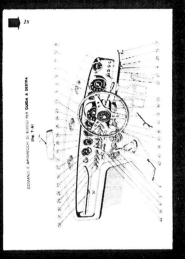

The first Ghibli manual, with a front cover finished in lime green; a colour you could buy the car in

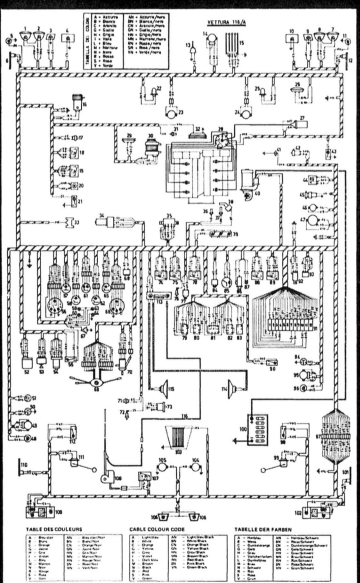

The Indy handbook enabled the driver to operate the switches in four languages

The mid-engined eights and sixes

Debuted at Geneva in 1971, Maserati exhibited what turned out to be the sensation of the show, the Bora. The faithful four-cam V8 in 4·7-litre form filled the rear half of the car and, at last, the factory like many other manufacturers, had gone 'mid-engine'. Located centrally, directly behind the driver, it was coupled to a ZF five-speed gearbox and substantial Borg and Beck clutch. The wheelbase was 104 inches and overall length just over 14 feet with a kerb weight (fuel tank, half full) of 3472 lb. The engine had an output of 310 bhp (DIN) at 6000 rpm and could propel the Bora effortlessly to over 160 mph. Skilfully, Giorgio Giugiaro of Ital Design had managed to come up with a stunning and practical design utilising the front half as an opening boot for luggage.

Finish, interior layout and function were accorded higher marks than usual for a Maserati by those who tested the car, although heating/ventilation and rear vision through the glass back light were criticised. Many drivers, however, had reservations concerning the Citroën pressurised hydraulics for the braking system. Also hydraulically operated were the head-lamps and driver's seat which coupled to the fully adjustable steering column gave a driving position suited to most.

Bora production became serious in 1972 and this included some right-hand drive examples imported by Citroën Cars who were then, of course, sole UK concessionaires. One of the more well known Boras in the UK must have been KBH 41K which was the 1972/73 slave to journalists and road testers being put through its paces by *Motor, Autocar, Autosport* and numerous other institutions. A concensus of their opinions would seem to have given very high marks for appearance, performance, handling and comfort, while against the model was its heavy fuel consumption around 11 mpg, heavy clutch and too sensitive brakes. Standing quarter miles could be achieved in 14·5 seconds by which time the Bora was travelling at 100 mph.

The satin-finished stainless roof panel was standard and certainly added to the car's already chunky appearance. I liked the press release from Citroën for the 1973 London Motor Show; 'The body was designed by the stylist Giugiaro and given those features indispensable for attaining a penetration coefficient to permit speeds of more than 175 mph. In spite of this, the driving compartment is comfortable enough for tall people'. What an amazingly versatile car to transport short and tall drivers!

In January 1976, Maserati management had thoughts of discontinuing the Bora but later in that year had a change of heart and promptly revised it with the 4·9 litre version of the V8.

Not a great departure in appearance from the Bora, Ital Design showed the Merak at Geneva in 1972. The Citroën SM V6 Maserati 2670 cc engine was used as the power unit for this new model, the reason being, I suspect, that the factory had many of these units lying around in anticipation of an ongoing relationship with Citroën. When that partnership failed and Citroën desired to sell off their Maserati holding, the Alfieri designed C.114 engine was increased to 2965 cc and placed in the middle of the Merak chassis. Outwardly, the twin aluminium struts at the rear had no glass enclosures, the stainless roof area was gone and the Merak construction relied on a rigid centre section from which everything was mounted. The gearbox was the SM five-speed, and the braking system was the same as the Bora. Weight was down to 3024 lb and although this new model did not have the power or ultimate speed of a Bora, it was nevertheless a sensible alternative. While the Bora was a spectacular, exotic car, the Merak never seemed to encourage such compliments. The finish was not as good as it might have been, and as usual the heating system was abysmal. Seemingly this had almost become a trait with each model from the Modena factory. The US versions of the Merak had a 'hump' at the rear to accommodate the normal size spare tyre, the very thin version not being acceptable to this market. It was not really acceptable anywhere, but merely intended for use in emergency and to get the owner on his travels.

Ground clearance was a criticism and certainly under hard braking the nose could kiss the ground. But roadholding was of the highest order and a Merak could be safely driven very fast through winding roads. Volume production commenced in 1973 and the factory offered this version until the Geneva Show in 1975 when the Merak SS was first shown. The great difference with this new version was the weight which had been decreased by over 100 lb and the V6 engine detailed to produce a further 30 bhp from the 3-litres. Again the chassis/body was unit construction in steel and these were made by small specialists in Turin. Instruments, layout and interior comforts were improved as was the overall quality of this more rapid, new model. Many considered the SS to be a more evenly balanced car than its sister, weight distribution had been altered from a ratio of 59/41 to 53/47 (rear/front). Tyres and wheel sizes were as the Bora with revised suspension settings to allow for the increased dimensions. At the Turin Show in late 1976, the Merak 2000 was on sale but exclusively for the Italian market. Political and economic problems were responsible for building such a car which could take advantage in some degree of the lower purchase and road tax for smaller capacity automobiles.

Bora production

Bora 4700/4900	Ital Design		
		1971	11 cars
		1972	162 cars
		1973	138 cars
		1974	72 cars
		1975	56 cars
		1976	6 cars
		1977	25 cars
		1978	25 cars
		TOTAL	495 cars

First chassis number AM117.002
First right hand drive version AM117.151

Merak production

Merak 3000	Ital Design		
		1972	17 cars
		1973	306 cars
		1974	312 cars
		1975	179 cars
		TOTAL	1309 cars
Merak 3000SS	Ital Design	1976	unknown
		1977	90 cars
		1978	134 cars
		TOTAL	224(?) cars
Merak 2000	Ital Design	1977	52 cars
		1978	50 cars
		TOTAL	102 cars

Doing what he liked best, on test with a Bora the last model Bertocchi drove before he left the Maserati factory to join De Tomaso

The prototype Bora being given a drink by Bertocchi. I was told the Chianti bottle did have water in it!

The second Bora built in 1971

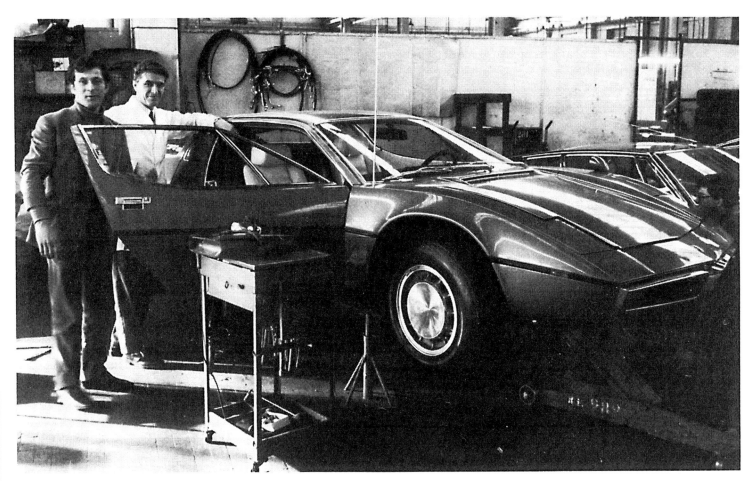

Ermanno Cozza showing a visiting gentleman the third Bora under construction at the factory in 1971

The same visitor now standing behind Ing. Alfieri who is busy advising some Citroën directors how to handle a Bora

The Bora was a superb Maserati which found a ready market world wide

Interior space was confined to two travellers with the glovebox for credit cards

On show at Geneva in 1972 proving accessibility to the mid-engine

Dimensions of the Bora on a postcard, illustrating the adjustable steering column, pedals and seat

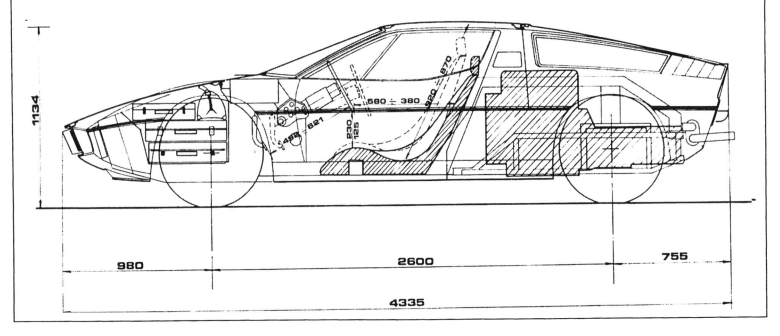

The factory interpretation of a 1978 Bora specifically for the
United States' market

Introduced at the Paris Salon of 1972, another Ital Design creation, the Maserati Merak

Still undergoing tests at the factory, the Bora (here to US specifications) now looked only faintly like its predecessor of six years earlier

The early Meraks were finished with a velour interior and arm rests which doubled as door pulls. Interior trim was not a quality feature

182

A large Merak mouth afforded adequate stowage space

Turin Show of 1976 with the Merak SS on the Maserati stand. The spoiler radically changed its frontal appearance but was necessary to keep this lightweight on the road

An horizontal grille was one of the outward distinguishing features of the SS which was some 150 kg lighter than its sister

For the Arabian market the factory added special bonnet and boot clips in the hope of sand sealing

Merak 2000 at the 1976 Turin Show

185

Side stripes had never been a Maserati fad until the 2-litre Merak

The interior of the Merak SS had a four spoke steering wheel, refined heater controls and improved instrument layout

The strength of the SS chassis lay in its steel construction which was nevertheless a fairly agricultural looking lump

The Merak SS V6 engine which was not renowned for its ease of access. One pulley is the alternator, the other is for the air conditioning. Note the Citroën servo system

2-litre Merak, also with the four spoke wheel and redesigned instruments

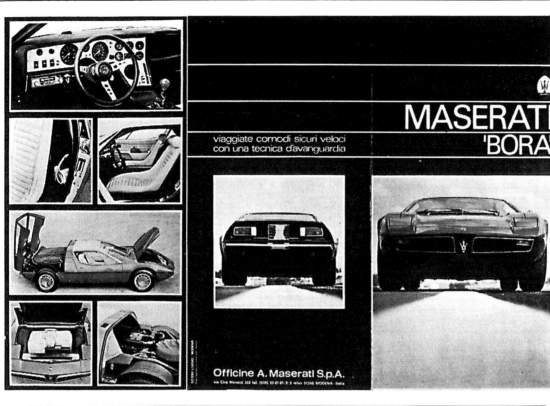

At last, the Bora! All the looks, style and go from the 4700 version of the V8 motor. The brochure endeavours to make the most of limited stowage space, and no girls were used for this brochure

MASERATI "BORA" GRAN TURISMO

SPECIFICATIONS

4.9 liter aluminum V-8 engine—Hemispherical combustion chambers—4 over head chain driven camshafts—4 dual throat Weber carburetors—5-speed synchromesh transmission—Fully independent front & rear suspension—Ventilated power disc brakes on all 4 wheels—Rack & pinion steering with damping—Steering wheel tilt & telescope—Steering wheel lock—Michelin steel-belted radial tires—Air conditioning—Fine leather upholstery—Power windows—Tinted glass—Speakers & electric antenna—Hydraulically operated driver seat & foot pedal cluster—Head rests—Electric rear window defroster—Dual horns—Light alloy wheels by "Campagnolo"—Electronically controlled adjustable side-view mirror—Electronic ignition system pointless—Heater/defroster with multi-speed blowers—Safety belts—Electric clock.

ENGINE (Central rear)
CYLINDER: V-8—90 degrees Hemispherical combustion chambers
BORE: 3.6968" (93.89 mm.)
STROKE: 3.5039" (88.99 mm.)
DISPLACEMENT: 300.87 cu. in. (4931 c.c.)
COMPRESSION RATIO: 8.5 to 1
MAX TORQUE: 308 ft. lbs. S.A.E. at 3500 r.p.m.
MAX POWER: 316 h.p. S.A.E. at 5000 r.p.m.
Four dual throat Weber carburetors
Four overhead chain driven camshafts
Electronic ignition system—pointless
CLUTCH: Single plate diaphragm spring with hydraulic control
GEAR BOX: 2-5 speed synchromesh & reverse
RATIOS: I-2.58—II-1.52—III-1.04—IV-0.845—V-0.74—reverse 2.86
AXLE RATIO: 4.22
CHASSIS: Integral body chassis construction
SUSPENSION: Fully independent front & rear suspension by coil spring, torsion bar & telescopic shock absorbers
BRAKES: Power brakes controlled by high pressure hydraulic system, Ventilated disc brakes on all 4 wheels, dual braking circuits independent for each axle
STEERING: Rack & pinion with dampers
STEERING WHEEL: Tilt & telescope
FUEL TANK CAPACITY: 25 U.S. gallons
WHEELS: 7.50 x 15—light alloy by Campagnolo
TIRES: 215/70 VR 15 Michelin steel belted radials

DIMENSIONS & WEIGHT

WHEEL BASE: 102.3"	(2598.4 mm.)
FRONT TRACK: 58"	(1473.2 mm.)
REAR TRACK: 56.9"	(1445.2 mm.)
OVERALL LENGTH: 171"	(4597.4 mm.)
OVERALL WIDTH: 69.6"	(1767.8 mm.)
OVERALL HEIGHT: 44.6"	(1132.8 mm.)
CURB WEIGHT: 3539 lbs.	(1605 kg.)
LUGGAGE SPACE: front compartment 9.5 cu. ft.	
BODY DESIGN: Giugiaro of Ital design	

The Maserati Trident
The symbol of a 60 year heritage...
the total uncompromising tribute to excellence
that is Maserati.

MASERATI AUTOMOBILES INCORPORATED

The Bora marketed by Maserati Automobiles Inc. to the US specifications included special impact bumpers front and rear. The stainless roof area has been blended in, unlike the earlier models, where it was a definite feature

MERAK

GRAN TURISMO: Body 2 seat head coupé 2+2 seats
Overall length mm. 4.335 170 in.
Overall width mm. 1.768 69.6 in.
Overall height mm. 1.134 44.6 in.
Approx. dry weight kg. 1.450 (3200 lbs.)
Approx. displacement c.c. 2.965 (181 cu. in.)

ENGINE: 6 cylinders 90 degrees V 90
Bore mm. 91.6 Stroke mm. 75 2965 c.c.
4 overhead camshafts (2 per bank of 3 cyls.) Compression ratio 8.75:1
Max torque 188 ft. lbs. 26 at 4000 r.p.m.
Max Power 182 h.p. S.A.E. at 6000 r.p.m.

TRANSMISSION: Hydraulically operated diaphragm clutch

CHASSIS & SUSPENSIONS: Chassis: Integral body chassis

DIMENSIONS AND WEIGHT: Wheel base mm. 2.600 (102.3 in.)

PERFORMANCES

OPTIONAL EXTRA EQUIPMENT: Air conditioning, electric

The factory announces its full range of cars, slipping the V6 Merak in with the reliable V8s

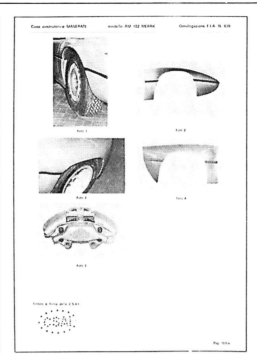

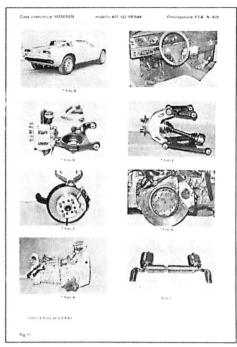

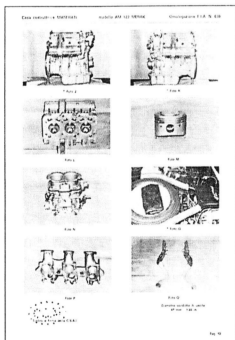

The FIA homologation paper on the
Tipo 122, or Merak, stating a minimum
build number of 500 examples from
September 1972

A 1974 sales brochure for the Merak.
This example has the velour covered
seats and electric clock!

190

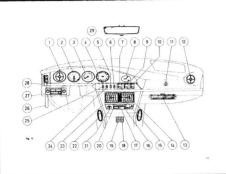

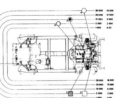

GENERAL CHARACTERISTICS

IMPIANTO DI CONDIZIONAMENTO — INSTALLATION DE CONDITIONNEMENT — CONDITIONING SYSTEM

ALIMENTAZIONE — ALIMENTATION — FEED

VELOCITA VETTURA — VITESSE DE LA VOITURE — CAR SPEED

Three languages for the Merak, with an encouraging introduction; 'Brakes and front lights work with engine running only'. I trust the handbrake was not an optional extra

Khamsin and Quattroporte II

Bertone's steel-built Khamsin was initially shown at the Turin Show in 1972, although as was normal with the factory, production did not commence until sometime afterwards, and in this case in 1974. Although announced as a 2 plus 2 coupé there was a complete lack of head, foot and leg room behind the rear seats rendering them impractical for passengers. The Khamsin was fitted with the controversial Citroën-patented hydraulics including the ingenious speed-related power steering. Unlike the Bora, clutch pressure was improved by having not only hydraulic operation but also an hydraulically assisted pedal ensuring short travel and very light pressure.

The coachwork was undoubtedly stunning in appearance; Bertone had blended the lines well to create a superbly beautiful new Maserati. The 'old' V8 propelled this model from 0–100 mph in 20 seconds, and pulling 6000 rpm in top meant a velocity of 140 mph. Consumption was 12 mpg and the Khamsin weighed in at 3584 lb, certainly lighter than its friends the Lamborghini Espada, Aston Martin V8 and Jensen Interceptor III.

Strangely the initial batch of right hand drive models were fitted with Borg-Warner three-speed automatic transmission. This did nothing for the car unless the owner of this then £13,000 toy happened to use it all the time in traffic. A more normal five-speed ZF gearbox was available.

As the factory press release for the Geneva Show said, 'it is a high class sporting car of reduced encombrement and more manageable in every journey condition'. The American magazine *Road & Track* said of the Khamsin in 1975, 'the Khamsin is an ego trip on wheels, but it's a trip most enthusiasts wouldn't mind taking.' The first year of production, 1974, saw 64 cars completed, commencing with chassis number AM120.002, while the first right hand drive model was AM120.0301.

Reverting to their 1963 model name, the Quattroporte II from Bertone was shown by this coachbuilder at the Turin Show in 1974. Unbeknown to anyone then, the car was, in fact, to remain a prototype never going into series production. The engine was the Tipo C.114, or Citroën SM unit, and as a V6 3-litre powering this five-seater, luxury saloon it was clearly inadequate. The car was too heavy with a dry weight of 3752 lb. It had all the heavy Citroën hydraulics and was certainly underpowered for the market it was aimed for. However Bertone's line was very clean and elegant. The interior was comfortable; wood veneers were used on the instrument panel, luxurious seating was included and the quality of fittings was high giving this model considerable style and refinement.

Sales of the Quattroporte II were confined to Arabia and South America although one was sold in Spain.

The second series Quattroporte II was announced at the Turin Show in 1976 and this time the factory installed the V8 engine in 4200 cc capacity. With ZF five-speed gearbox, ZF power steering and Girling disc brakes, production was to commence in September 1977. This, in fact, did not materialize as several production problems were encountered and at the end of that year the factory informed customers that delivery of the V8 version would not be until 1978. However, at the end of 1978 no V8 Quattroportes had left the production line.

Khamsin production

Khamsin 4900	Bertone	1974	64 cars
		1975	102 cars
		1976	26 cars
		1977	80 cars
		1978	80 cars
		TOTAL	352 cars

Quattroporte II production

Quattroporte II 3000 (V6)	Bertone	1975	002	1 car
		1976	004 006	2 cars
		1977	008 010	2 cars
		TOTAL		5 cars

Five cars built, 002 retained by the factory as the prototype, 004 sold to Spain

Geneva Show 1975 on the Bertone stand and the new Khamsin has now entered production

A lonely Bora being overtaken by the new Khamsin model on a healthy production line in September 1976

A beautiful front-engine Maserati harking back to Ghibli days

An additional air vent in the nose, US regulation bumpers and recessed traffic indicators distinguish the 1977 Khamsin

The upright rear glass panel with the new shape forcing the light cluster lower down on the body line

Doing what comes naturally with a Maserati. This is a 1976
Khamsin being exercised

First shown at Turin in 1974, the second edition of the
Quattroporte by Bertone

Interior of the original Quattroporte II from Bertone as shown on this coachbuilder's stand at the 1975 Paris Show

Certainly made in the grand touring manner although still a prototype here

195

The production line at the factory in April 1977 and the new Quattroporte begins to get into gear

Everything about the revised Quattroporte II has changed
since 1974 including the size of the bonnet!

The 1978 production of the four door will hopefully be ready
to satisfy customers in 1979. Wheel design was altered for
the 1979 Geneva Show

KHAMSIN MASERATI

The new Khamsin was displayed in this 1973 brochure with appalling green carpeting. An optional extra was the right-hand drive conversion

I think the 1974 Khamsin brochure was developed on a theme originating from an Italian poet. He did, however, begin to use the word Legend, and acknowledge Maserati's associations of long ago

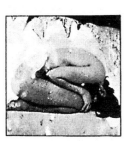

Meet her, one day,
as in a dream.
Recognize her
by her exalting lines,
discover the bold principles
which give her life,
capable of re-inventing
a traditional concept,
bringing it up to date,
setting it even now in
the future.
Like the wind,
this everlasting wind,
ever changing,
even now.

Hydraulic power steering with
powered centering. Feel
increases progressively with
road speed.
Independent suspension all round
Self locking differential
Hydraulic high-pressure power brakes
Hydraulic servo-operated clutch
Air conditioning
Leather interior.
Options: - automatic transmission
right hand steering.
Designed by Bertone.

KHAMSIN MASERATI

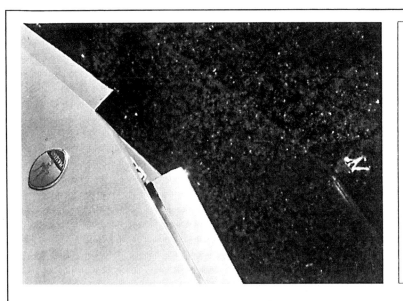

MASERATI
MERAK**SS**

The SS version of the Merak was shown to good effect in this stylised version of love's young dream although in the same brochure the Quattroporte II's specifications were given

Two different sales brochures, one red, one blue (over page),
were produced with the original Tipo 26 badge on the front
cover in the late 1970s. The complete range of cars on offer
by Maserati were credited in these quality productions.
Above are the Merak details and Khamsin power train while
overleaf are more Merak and Quattroporte II features

-QUATTROPORTE- MASERATI

MASERATI «MERAK/SS»

-MERAK/SS- MASERATI

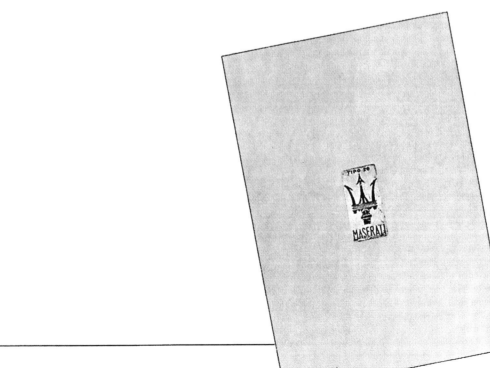

Dated 1974 this brochure was for the first series Quattroporte II which as shown here never got into serious production. An uprated and sorted-out production version became a reality for 1978

CARATTERISTICHE GENERALI				GENERAL CHARACTERISTICS				CARACTERISTIQUES GENERALES			
GRAN TURISMO: 5 posti - Velocita massima oltre		Km/h	200	**GRAND TOURING:** 5 seats - Max speed over Km/h 200 (over 124 M.P.H.)				**GRAND TOURISME:** 5 places - Maximum vitesse		plus de Km/h	200
CARROZZERIA: Berlina				**BODY:** Sedan				**CARROSSERIE:** Berline			
Lunghezza massima		mm.	5130	Overall length		mm. 5130 (inches 201.9)			Longueur		mm.	5130
Larghezza massima		mm.	1870	Overall width		mm. 1870 (inches 73.6)			Largeur		mm.	1870
Altezza massima		mm.	1370	Overall height		mm. 1370 (inches 53.9)			Hauteur		mm.	1370
Bagagliaio		mc.	0.75	Luggage compartment		mc. 0.75 (cu.ft. 25)			Coffre a bagages		mc.	0.75
MOTORE: 6 cilindri a V - 90				**ENGINE:** 6 cylinder V-90				**MOTEUR:** 6 cylindres V 90			
Alesaggio		mm.	91.6	Bore		mm. 91.6 (inches 3.6)			Alesage		mm.	91.6
Corsa		mm.	75	Stroke		mm. 75 (inches 2.95)			Course		mm.	75
Cilindrata totale		cc.	2965	Cubic capacity		cc. 2965 (c inches 180.9)			Cylindree totale		cc.	2965
Rapporto di compressione		8.8 : 1	8.8 : 1	Compression ratio			8.8 : 1		Rapport de compression			8.8 : 1

Quattro alberi a cammes in testa - camera combustione emisferica. Tre carburatori doppio corpo - lubrificazione forzata a filtraggio totale, radiatore olio. Raffred. ad acqua con pompa centrif. Radiatore con due ventilatori elettrici.

TRASMISSIONE: Trazione anteriore - Trasmissioni omocinetiche - frizione monodisco a secco con servoassistenza idraulica Cambio a 5 marce sincronizzate piu retromarcia.

TELAIO: Carrozzeria autoportante: telaio a piattaforma

Passo		mm.	3070
Carreggiata anteriore		mm.	1520
Carreggiata posteriore		mm.	1490

SOSPENSIONI ANT. E POST. Idropneumatiche a 4 ruote indipendenti - correttori d'assetto automatici. Possibilità di variare a piacimento l'altezza da terra.

FRENI: 4 freni a disco a doppio circuito con ripartizione automatica in funzione al carico.

STERZO: A cremagliera, ad assistenza idraulica variabile in funzione velocita richiamo asservito.

SERBATOIO CARBURANTE: Capacita totale	Lt.	100
consumo Norme CUNA x 100 Km	Lt.	12

RUOTE: Cerchi da 6"

PNEUMATICI:	Michelin 205 70 VR 15

A CORREDO DI SERIE: Aria condizionata, vetri atermici azzurati, tendine frangisole, radio con mangianastri, vetri elettrici, servosterzo. Lunotto termico.

A RICHIESTA: Interno in pelle - tetto apribile elettricamente

* I presenti dati hanno un valore indicativo

MASERATI preferisce AGIP

Four overhead camshafts - Hemispherical combustion chamber. Three twinbody carburettors - Forced lubrication with total filtering. Water cooling system by centrifugal pump. Radiator with electrically controlled fans.

TRANSMISSION: Front wheel drive - Constant velocity transmissions - Single dry plate clutch with hydraulic control - Five synchronized gears and reverse.

CHASSIS: Body integral with frame and support chassis

Wheel base		mm. 3070 (inches 120.8)
Ground level track-front		mm. 1520 (inches 59.8)
Ground level track-rear		mm. 1490 (inches 58.6)

FRONT AND REAR SUSPENSION: Hidropneumatic suspension with 4 independent wheels - Automatic leveling system tabs - Possibility of changing the road clearance when necessary.

BRAKES: 4 twin circuit disc brakes with automatic distribution of load.

STEERING: Rack and pinion steering wheel with variable hydraulic servo according to the speed and interlocked returning.

FUEL TANK: Total capacity	100 liters (imp g. 22) (USA g. 26.5)
Consumption as per CUNA regulations each 100 KMS 12 liters (20 m.p.g.)	

WHEELS: Rims 6"

TIRES:	Michelin 205 70 VR 15

STANDARD EQUIPMENT: Air conditioning, tinted electric windows, sun window shades, radio with stereo tapes, electrically controlled windows, power steering

OPTIONAL EQUIPMENT: Leather inner upholstery, electr. control sliding roof

* The above data are only indicative and may change as deemed necessary

MASERATI likes most AGIP

Quatre arbres a cames en tête - Culasse hemisphérique - Trois carburateurs double corps - Graissage sous pression avec nettoyage total - Refroidissement par eau par moyen d'une pompe centr. - Rad. avec vent. commandes electriq.

TRANSMISSION: Traction avant - Transmission homocinetique - Embrayage monodisque a sec avec servo commande hydraulique - Boite de vitesses a 5 vitesses synchronisees et marche arriere.

CHASSIS: Carrosserie integrée au chassis: chassis à plaque-support

Empattement		mm.	3070
Voie avant		mm.	1520
Voie arriere		mm.	1490

SUSPENSION AV. ET AR.: Hydropneumatiques a quatre roues indépendantes - Dispositif de variation de la hauteur libre sous la voiture.

FREINS: Quatre freins a disque et a double circuit et répartition automatique de pression selon la charge.

DIRECTION: A cremaillère et commande servo-hydraulique variable suivant la vitesse, rappel asservi.

RESERVOIR D'ESSENCE: Capacite totale lt. 100	
Consommation suivant Reglements CUNA lt. 12 chaque 100 Km	

ROUES: Jantes 6"

PNEUMATIQUES:	Michelin 205 70 VR 15

SERIE: Climatisation, glaces teintées et à commande électrique, rideaux pare-soleil, radio-cassette, direction avec dispositif servo

SUR DEMANDE: Intérieur en cuir - Toit ouvrant electriquement

* Les caractéristiques ci-dessus sont fournies seulement a indicatif

MASERATI choisit AGIP

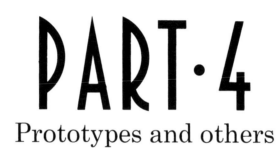

PART·4

Prototypes and others

A V8 carburettor engine inside a mock-up body built in 1961.
The chassis was a 3500 (Tipo 101) and the engine was given
Tipo number 104 a direct descendent of the 5000GT (Tipo
103)

It is difficult to know the correct number for this prototype
but the factory titled it a Tipo 108

The finished model of the lower one on the previous page by Touring of Milan

Intricate coackwork for the rear light cluster and absence of
side flashings enhanced this coupé's appearance

A 3·7 litre six cylinder injection engine in a handsome coupé. But what is it?

The rear end begins to look like a Quattroporte, is it by Carrozzeria Frua?

The car has now changed its colour and side indicators on the wing have been added

206

The snap-on exhaust trims have gone, but reflectors beneath the Sebring type rear lights have appeared

A 3500GTI by Touring of Milan in 1960. Or is it?

The factory called this a Tipo 104 experimental. But nobody remembers it!

Is this the same car pictured at the factory in 1960, overleaf?
(This photograph was taken in 1962)

The rear quarter still resembling his
Ghibli, Ghia could not persuade
Maserati to adopt his new design shown
at Turin in 1970

GHIA presents:

" S I M U N "

The design of the "Simun" is quite different from the one of "Ghibli", pre-
sented last year at the Turin Show as, in this case, GHIA wanted to create
a car with marked sport characteristics but, in the meantime, with an extre
mely stylish line.

The essential characteristic of this car is, with no doubt, the side view:
the large windows joining without interruption the windshield to the rear
window offer a perfect visibility both to the driver and to passengers. More
over, from the same design of the side window has been drawn the lid of the
gas tank cap.

The upper line of the fender, very tighten in the hood and door side, has been
interrupted by a relief which stresses the rear wheels presence: here it is,
the old and traditional styling detail, that only by a right proportion can get
interesting and new.

The front side is divided in two air intakes shown up by a black grille : the
upper air intake is framed by a small chromium-plated flat band having on
the center the Maserati badge. The bumper frames the lower air intake,
where the parking lights are placed.

Headlights are self concealing and, in order to lighten their lid, instead of
making it only in one piece, was decided to divide it in two fins.

In the rear view, the "Simun" shows a peculiar trapezoidal shape.

As far as the interior is concerned, we have to notice the dashboard, which
is designed like the one of aeroplanes, with the same functionality.

One very interesting detail: on the dashboard there are some warning lights
which advise the driver when rear lights do not work.

Specification

Maserati engine, 8 cylinders, 4200 cc.
Wheelbase 2600 mm., front track 1480 mm., rear track 1480 mm.

Press release from Carrozzeria Ghia on
his Simun, a car based on the 4200 V8
Maserati chassis

The factory decided this Giugiaro designed Maserati
Boomerang could not be put into series production

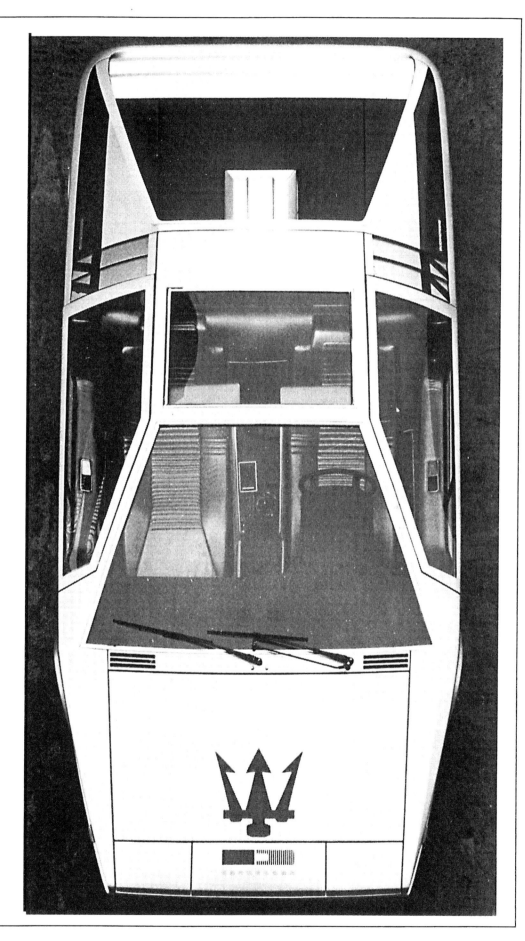

Even increasing the size of the Trident symbol did not convince the management at Modena

211

In its final form, the Boomerang as shown at Geneva in 1972.
The car remained the property of Ital Design

The cleanest interior of any
Maserati, and certainly
sensational

Maserati coupé by Ital based on the 4·7 litre V8 Indy chassis

Shown at Turin in 1973, Maserati did not put the Ital coupé
into production

The interior like, many Giugiaro designs, was luxurious and
stimulating on this Indy based car

215

The original drawing for the Maserati Medici by Ital Design, a
car which was intended for an American customer

The second Maserati Medici displayed by Ital Design at the
1976 Paris Salon

It was reported that this second Medici was purchased by
Shah of Persia at the Paris Salon. I will resist reporting the
incredible price

Cloth interior with a seating capacity for six. This first
Medici was exhibited at 1974 Turin Show

The interior was greatly changed and the second model
became a normal four seater

Bora Competitizion commissioned by J. Thepenier the French
Maserati importer. It is seen at the Modena test track in its
initial form

Intended for the GT class at the 1973 Le Mans 24-Hours the Bora could not be homologated as the 500-cars-a-year rule had not been achieved by the factory. Neither could it enter the prototype class as it was over 3-litres

Thepenier originally planned a two-car team for Le Mans but the entire project never really took off. This is chassis number 3001

A spider Merak created by Maserati distributors, Steering Wheel Inc. in Florida. This version had a one piece removable top but storage of the panel was a problem

Next came the Targa Merak by Steering Wheel Inc. The chassis was strengthened at the sills and windscreen pillars gusseted on the seam. The car is a 1975 model

Kyalami

While some thought the new Khamsin was intended to replace the Indy, it, in fact, filled the vacant Ghibli market which left the factory with no genuine 2 plus 2 coupé. One of De Tomaso's first manoeuvres once in control of the Trident was to give his Longchamp to Carrozzeria Frua, in Turin, for some sheet metal modifications front and rear. While Frua was busy blending in the new, the factory were modifying the De Tomaso chassis to house the Maserati V8 *motore* in place of the American Ford V8 which the Longchamp was using.

Obviously this new model had no Citroën fittings in its original construction, being pure Italian in make-up, although a 'bitsa'. With the modifications completed the Kyalami was exhibited at the 1976 Geneva Show, where it was not exactly recognised as a new model by the press. By the Turin Show, later in the same year, many improvements and modifications had been made to this two-door coupé although it still resembled a Longchamp in outward appearance. Series production at the De Tomaso factory was scheduled to commence in December 1976, but this new model was not available until late 1977. The Kyalami could not be said to be a Maserati development of any kind; it initially proved that De Tomaso could integrate his two car factories which is only what he had announced when he took control.

The first Kyalami had chassis number AM129.002. Some fifty 4200 Kyalami's were built in 1977 and again in 1978, plus ten 4900s in 1978 also.

The early version of the Kyalami thinly disguised, and still looking like a Longchamp, at the beginning of 1976

 224 Front sidelights and indicators incorporated are now in the substantial front bumper. Beneath is a marginal air scoop.

The Kyalami looked razor sharp and was a typical Frua creation

A press sheet announcing the 4·2 litre-Kyalami for the 1976 Geneva Show

"KYALAMI" MASERATI 4200 cc. 2+2

MOTEUR (antérieur)

— Nombre de cylindres	8 en V à 90 degrés
— Alésage	88 mm.
— Course	85 mm.
— Cylindrée	4136 cc.
— Rapport de compression	8,5 : l.
— Couple maxi	40 Kgm. à 3800 tr/mn.
— Puissance	265 HP Din à 6000 tr/mn.

Quatre carburateurs double corps - Culasse hémisphérique - Quatre arbres à cames en tête - Alternateur 650 Watt. - Batterie 12 V. 60 Amp/h - Allumage électrique - Refroidissement de l'eau avec pompe centrifuge - Lubrification forcée - filtrage total.

TRANSMISSION

— Embrayage	Monodisco à sec et commande hydraulique
— Boîte de vitesses	ZF à 5 vitesses synchronisées et marche arrière
— Rapports	I - 2,99 II - 1,90 III - 1,32 IV - 1 V - 0,89 R - 2,70
— Transmission	Couple hypoidale 1 : 3,54
— Sur demande	Boîte automatique

CHASSIS - SUSPENSIONS

— Chassis	à structure portante, ensemble chassis-carrosserie
— Suspensions avant et arrière	à roues indépendantes avec ressort hélicoidaux barre stabilisatrice et amortisseurs téléscopiques
— Freins	à disque ventilés flottants auto-centrants, avec commande hydraulique - servofrein à depression - double circuit
— Direction	assistée hydraulique
— Volant	règlable en hauteur
— Réservoir essence	Capacité totale 100 lt. - Consommation aux 100 Km. 12,8 lt. (norme Cuna)
— Roues	7,50 x 15 en alliage léger
— Pneumatiques	205/70 VR 15 XDX Tub.

Conditionateur d'air.

DIMENSIONS ET POIDS

— Empattement	2600 mm.
— Voie avant	1530 mm.
— Voie arrière	1530 mm.
— Longueur	4580 mm.
— Largeur	1850 mm.
— Hauteur	1270 mm.
— Poids à vide en ordre de marche	1550 Kg.
— Coffre à bagages arrière	0,4 mt.^{3}
— Carrosserie dessin « FRUA »	Coupé 2+2 places

PERFORMANCES

— Vitesse maxi	240 Km/h.

* Les caractéristiques ci-dessus sont fournies seulement à titre indicatif. L'Officine Alfieri Maserati se réserve de les modifier sans préavis.

OFFICINE ALFIERI MASERATI S.p.A. - AUTOMOBILI (MODENA Italia)

An early arrival at the 1976 Turin Show. Wheels and bumpers
have been revised

227

228

ACKNOWLEDGEMENTS

I wish to express my thanks to the many people who have assisted me with information on Maseratis over many years—material has arrived from all over the world.

For their continued support I want to thank the Maserati factory—in spite of their many ups and downs, the factory goes on—and in particular Ermanno Cozza.

This book mostly concerns Maserati's Orsi period—I have received pleasant co-operation from both Omer Orsi and his son, Adolfo Orsi Jr. Thank you.

Corrado Millanta deserves special thanks. He loaned many photographs for our first Maserati book—this time we have not made so much use of his material—nevertheless his assistance has been invaluable.

Photographs were supplied by *Automobile Review*, Carrozzeria Bertone SpA, Tom Clark, David Cohen, Peter Coltrin, E. Dibbern, Guy Foog, Foto Botti & Pincelli, Fototechnica, Carrozzeria Frua, Carrozzeria Ghia, Egon Hofer, Ital Design, Minoru Kawamoto, Richard Kreischer, Manfred Lampe, Musee Henri Malarte, Jean-Francois Marchet, Hans Matti, Paul Merrigan, Corrado Millanta, National Motor Museum, Robert Neunreiter, Stanley Nowak, Tim Parker, Carrozzeria Pininfarina, Publifoto, Boris Subbotin, Hans Tanner and, of course, Officine Alfieri Maserati SpA. Other photographs come from the collections of Richard Crump and Rob de la Rive Box.

All the Maserati factory brochures, handbooks and manuals come from the collection of Richard Crump.

These factory brochures, handbooks and manuals were chosen as being a representative selection since 1946. That there are others is well known, but in some cases reproduction would have been too poor to give any pleasure because of their original state.

229